Cambridge Elements ≡

Elements in England in the Early Medieval World
edited by
Megan Cavell
University of Birmingham
Rory Naismith
University of Cambridge
Winfried Rudolf
University of Göttingen
Emily V. Thornbury
Yale University

MULTILINGUALISM IN EARLY MEDIEVAL BRITAIN

Lindy Brady
Edge Hill University

CAMBRIDGE
UNIVERSITY PRESS

Shaftesbury Road, Cambridge CB2 8EA, United Kingdom

One Liberty Plaza, 20th Floor, New York, NY 10006, USA

477 Williamstown Road, Port Melbourne, VIC 3207, Australia

314–321, 3rd Floor, Plot 3, Splendor Forum, Jasola District Centre,
New Delhi – 110025, India

103 Penang Road, #05–06/07, Visioncrest Commercial, Singapore 238467

Cambridge University Press is part of Cambridge University Press & Assessment,
a department of the University of Cambridge.

We share the University's mission to contribute to society through the pursuit of
education, learning and research at the highest international levels of excellence.

www.cambridge.org
Information on this title: www.cambridge.org/9781009467896

DOI: 10.1017/9781009275811

First published 2023

A catalogue record for this publication is available from the British Library

ISBN 978-1-009-46789-6 Hardback
ISBN 978-1-009-27585-9 Paperback
ISSN 2632-203x (online)
ISSN 2632-2021 (print)

Multilingualism in Early Medieval Britain

Elements in England in the Early Medieval World

DOI: 10.1017/9781009275811
First published online: September 2023

Lindy Brady
Edge Hill University

Author for correspondence: Lindy Brady, Lindy.Brady@edgehill.ac.uk

Abstract: In the words of its own historians, pre-Norman Britain held five languages and four peoples. Yet in modern scholarship, Old English is too often studied separately from the other languages that surrounded it. This Element offers a comprehensive synthesis of the evidence from the pre-Norman period that situates Old English as one of several living languages that together formed the basis of a vibrant oral and written literary culture in early medieval Britain. Each section centres around a key thematic topic and is illustrated through a series of memorable case studies that encapsulate the extent to which multilingualism appeared in every facet of life in early medieval Britain: religious and scholarly; political and military; economic and cultural; intellectual and artistic. The Element makes an overall argument for the dynamic extent of transcultural literary and linguistic culture in early medieval Britain before the arrival of the Normans.

Keywords: multilingual, transcultural, early medieval Britain, Old English, Celtic languages

ISBNs: 9781009467896 (HB), 9781009275859 (PB), 9781009275811 (OC)
ISSNs: 2632-203x (online), 2632-2021 (print)

Contents

Introduction: Multilingualism in Early Medieval Britain

In the early eighth century, the Northumbrian historian Bede wrote: 'at the present time, there are five languages in Britain … these are the English, British, Irish, Pictish, as well as the Latin languages; through the study of the scriptures, Latin is in general use among them all'.[1] One hundred years later, the British author of the *Historia Brittonum* described how Britain held four peoples, 'the Irish, the Picts, the Saxons and the British'.[2] It was clear to those who lived in early medieval Britain that Old English, the precursor of the modern English spoken around the world today, was one of four vernacular languages (native tongues) spoken and that those who spoke it were one of four *gentes* (peoples) to inhabit the island. As the centuries passed, they would be joined by Norse-speaking groups of Scandinavians collectively known as Vikings and the French-speaking Normans, among others to leave their linguistic mark on the island. Early medieval Britain was a multilingual space: a place where multiple languages were in use simultaneously. Britain's various tongues did not merely coexist alongside one another, but also frequently overlapped within the same spheres: religious, intellectual, political, economic, and visually, whether on the pages of manuscripts or inscribed on stone monuments for passers-by to see.

Yet Old English has too often been treated as if it existed separately from the other languages that were spoken in early medieval Britain,[3] a phenomenon caused in large part by the rise of nationalism from the early modern period onwards.[4] This means that materials from different linguistic traditions are rarely studied together,[5] and while a handful of excellent individual studies have explored aspects of multilingualism in early medieval Britain, they have largely focused on one linguistic relationship at a time: Old English and Old Norse,[6] Old English and Welsh,[7] Old Irish and Welsh,[8] Old English and Latin,[9]

---

[1] Colgrave and Mynors, *Bede's Ecclesiastical History of the English People*, i.1, 16–17.

[2] Morris, *Nennius*, 59 and 18.

[3] Early exceptions include Hector Munro and Nora Kershaw Chadwick, and Kenneth Hurlstone Jackson; see Lapidge, *Interpreters of Early Medieval Britain*. More recently, see Callander, *Dissonant Neighbours*; Edmonds, *Gaelic Influence in the Northumbrian Kingdom*; Brady, *Origin Legends*; and Ireland, *The Gaelic Background of Old English Poetry before Bede*.

[4] Geary, *Myth of Nations*, 15–40.

[5] Exceptions include Trotter, *Multilingualism in Later Medieval Britain*; Tyler, *Conceptualizing Multilingualism in England*; Jefferson and Putter, *Multilingualism in Medieval Britain (c. 1066–1520)*; Schrijver, *Language Contact and the Origins of the Germanic Languages*; and Clarke and Ní Mhaonaigh, *Medieval Multilingual Manuscripts*.

[6] Townend, *Language and History in Viking Age England*.

[7] Higley, *Between Languages: The Uncooperative Text in Early Welsh and Old English Nature Poetry*; and Callander, *Dissonant Neighbours*.

[8] Sims-Williams, *Irish Influence on Medieval Welsh Literature*.

[9] Stephenson and Thornbury, *Latinity and Identity in Anglo-Saxon Literature*; Gallagher and Tinti, *The Languages of Early Medieval Charters*.

Middle English and French.[10] The implications of isolating Old English from its insular counterparts are not just a matter of scholarly semantics. In a 2014 speech during the lead-up to Brexit, for instance, then-UKIP leader Nigel Farage stated that 'this country in a short space of time has frankly become unrecognisable . . . it is the fact in many parts of England you don't hear English spoken any more. This is not the kind of community we want to leave to our children and grandchildren'.[11] Farage's xenophobic speech restricted 'English' identity to native speakers and implied that the presence of multiple languages in England was a recent change, and in his view, a change for the worse.

Yet as we have seen, Bede's characterisation of Britain's linguistic landscape as composed of four vernaculars with Latin as a shared *lingua franca* meant that the island was perceived as a multilingual space in the early medieval period. This Element outlines the web of multilingual connections within early medieval Britain as understood and experienced by its inhabitants, offering a comprehensive synthesis of the evidence from the pre-Norman period that situates Old English as one of several living languages which together formed the basis of a vibrant oral and written literary culture. The volume explores exchanges between the vernacular languages of early medieval Britain (Old English, Irish Gaelic, Pictish, and British), as well as Old Norse, which entered the island during the Viking Age, and Latin, concluding with a look at the impact of Norman French from the eleventh century onwards. (There is not space to discuss Ireland or continental Europe, but the conclusions drawn here extend to these regions as well.)[12] Each section centres around a key thematic topic and is illustrated through a series of memorable case studies that encapsulate the extent to which multilingualism appeared in every facet of life. This Element follows the ebbs and flows of contact patterns between various vernaculars over time, making an overall argument for the dynamic extent of transcultural literary and linguistic culture in Britain before the arrival of the Normans.

A language is a structured system that groups of sentient beings use to communicate with one another. All of the languages spoken in early medieval Britain – as was the case throughout most of the medieval European west, with some notable exceptions such as Finnish, Hungarian, and Basque – are descended from the same ancestral language, and therefore belong to the same language family, known as Indo-European. When a group of people moved to a new location, their language naturally diverged over time from that spoken in the place that they had left. When two groups diverge enough to have different

---

[10] Wogan-Browne et al., *The French of England, c.1100–c.1500.*   [11] Sparrow, 'Nigel Farage'.
[12] Tinti, *Europe and the Anglo-Saxons*; Mullen, *Southern Gaul and the Mediterranean.*

speech patterns or vocabulary but are still largely intelligible to one another, their languages are referred to as dialects. When they are no longer largely intelligible, they have become different languages. Scholars use the terminology of genealogy to describe the relationships between languages: two languages may have 'descended' from a common 'ancestor', or 'evolved' until they 'diverged' from one another. 'Related' languages belong to the same language 'family' and can share varying degrees of closeness depending upon how far up the 'family tree' their shared ancestor exists.

The five languages named by Bede represent three branches within the broader Indo-European language family.[13] Latin belongs to the Italic branch and is the ancestor of modern Romance languages such as Spanish, Italian, and French. The latter is also partly descended from Norman French, whose speakers came to Britain in 1066. British – which would eventually split into the Welsh, Cornish, and now-extinct Pictish languages – and Irish Gaelic are Celtic languages. Old English belongs to the Germanic language family, which includes such languages as German, Flemish, and Dutch in addition to Old Norse, the language spoken by the Vikings and the ancestor of modern Scandinavian languages like Icelandic, Norwegian, Danish, and Swedish. Our journey through the multilingualism of early medieval Britain will also touch on other languages spoken there at various points, such as Frisian and Greek, but will focus mostly on the languages recognised by those who lived in early medieval Britain as having been spoken by major groups of permanent inhabitants.

The written history of Britain by Britons began with the arrival of the Romans and Latinate culture to the island,[14] which was inhabited from the Palaeolithic period, but not continuously.[15] Permanent settlement began around 9,000 years ago after the end of the last Ice Age.[16] The precise date at which a recognisable 'Celtic' culture and language family emerged is uncertain, though migration from Gaul during the Bronze Age has been suggested as influential.[17] Depictions of the island by classical Greek and Latin authors described its inhabitants using terminology cognate with Celtic languages,[18] and certainly by the Iron Age,[19] people speaking the ancestor of the Celtic language family

---

[13] Kapović, *The Indo-European Language*.

[14] For references to Britain in classical and late antique texts, see Merrills, *History and Geography in Late Antiquity*.

[15] Darvill, *Prehistoric Britain*; Pettitt and White, *The British Palaeolithic*.

[16] Conneller, *The Mesolithic in Britain*.

[17] Patterson et al., 'Large-scale migration into Britain during the Middle to Late Bronze Age'.

[18] Cunliffe, *The Ancient Celts*, 2–14 and 29–52.

[19] Haselgrove and Pope, *The Earlier Iron Age in Britain and the Near Continent*; Haselgrove and Moore, *The Later Iron Age in Britain and Beyond*; Cunliffe, *The Ancient Celts*.

(known as Proto-Celtic or common Celtic) and associated with the La Tène material culture lived in Britain.[20] By 43 CE, when southern Britain was annexed and subsequently invaded as part of the Roman Empire under the emperor Claudius, the island was inhabited by speakers of several Celtic languages: Pictish and Gaelic were spoken in modern-day Scotland, British in the Old North and southern Britain, as well as Gaelic in pockets of what is now Wales. For the next 350 years, Britain south of the Firth of Forth was a Roman province.[21] The Roman impact on all facets of British life was significant,[22] not least on multilingualism. The Romans brought with them a new language and alphabet – Latin, both written and spoken – whose influence persisted long past their departure in the fifth century.[23]

During the fifth and sixth centuries, the Anglo-Saxons – loose groupings of Germanic-speaking peoples from the continent – came to Britain.[24] The language they spoke after their arrival is known as Old English. Bede described how 'they came from three very powerful Germanic tribes, the Saxons, Angles, and Jutes',[25] and this perception of political division despite a common language played a crucial role in the history of early medieval Britain. The Angles, Saxons, and Jutes formed many separate kingdoms after their arrival, and it is important to note that something approaching an 'English' identity did not emerge until a much later time period. Nigel Farage's speech quoted above is one of many which aptly illustrate the dangers of imagining that an unbroken, monolithic concept of supposed 'English' identity can be extended back until the fifth century. Although the phrase was already current in pre-Norman Britain, not all of the Angles, Saxons, and Jutes living there would have thought of themselves primarily as 'Anglo-Saxons': they were more likely to consider themselves first as Northumbrian, or Bernician, or as an inhabitant of their home village. But they were aware that they shared a language with those of their neighbours who did not speak British, Pictish, or Gaelic.[26] This Element therefore uses the phrase 'Anglo-Saxon' to denote the Angles, Saxons, and Jutes as a group who shared a language but not political cohesiveness, in order to avoid giving the false and dangerous impression that a unified 'English' identity can be projected back to post-Roman Britain.

---

[20] Harding, *The Archaeology of Celtic Art*.

[21] The extent of Roman-controlled territory was marked by two walls running West–East across Britain: Hadrian's Wall (at the Solway Firth) and the Antonine Wall (at the Firth of Forth).

[22] Salway, *A History of Roman Britain*; Bédoyère, *Roman Britain*; Fleming, *Britain after Rome*.

[23] Gerrard, *The Ruin of Roman Britain*.

[24] For good surveys of the early period, see Yorke, *Kings and Kingdoms of Early Anglo-Saxon England*; and Naismith, *Early Medieval Britain*.

[25] Colgrave and Mynors, *Bede's Ecclesiastical History of the English People*, i.15, 51.

[26] See Hines, 'Who Did the Anglo-Saxons Think They Were?'.

By the time Bede's *Historia Ecclesiastica* was written in the early eighth century, Britain's multilingual landscape consisted of five languages: Old English, spoken in southern Britain; Pictish, spoken in what is now Scotland; Gaelic, spoken in what are now Scotland and Wales; British, spoken in southern Britain and the Old North; and Latin, spoken throughout the island. The next stage in Britain's linguistic evolution involved concurrent, though unrelated, additions and subtractions. During roughly the same time as the arrival of the Vikings, from the late eighth century onwards, the Pictish language was also vanishing.[27] The Pictish people lived in northern Britain, in the geographical region now known as Scotland, and spoke a Celtic language like British, though very little written material in Pictish survives.[28] In the early medieval period, the kingdom of the Picts existed alongside the Gaelic kingdom of the Dál Riata, which encompassed territory in both Britain and Ireland. Over time, Gaelic influence and political power increased until the Pictish kingdom and language were either conquered by or absorbed into a broader Gaelic kingdom within the region that would become known first as Alba and later as Scotland. The Pictish language and political identity vanished by the mid-ninth century, and the process of Gaelicisation was complete by the eleventh century. A similar process of linguistic erosion took place in the southwest in what is now Cornwall, where British (which would eventually split into Welsh and Cornish) was subsumed by the expansion of Old English speakers into that region and the absorption of Cornwall into Anglo-Saxon England. The loss of Cornish was a much more gradual process than that of Pictish: the last native speaker died in the eighteenth century, and Cornish is now a revived language.

Another significant movement of a people into Britain was that of groups of Scandinavians, known collectively as Vikings, beginning in the late eighth century.[29] The Old Norse word *víkingr* seems often to have meant something like 'pirate' and has become used as a shorthand for groups of sea-based peoples who emerged from the Scandinavian regions and raided widely across the medieval world from roughly the eighth to eleventh centuries, eventually forming new settlements in the places that they had initially attacked.[30] These 'Vikings' spoke the Germanic language of Old Norse, which was related to Old English. In Britain, the Viking Age began with raids carried out on coastal communities during the summers in the late eighth and early ninth centuries. By the mid-ninth century, the Vikings were 'overwintering', allowing them to carry

---

[27] Fraser, *From Caledonia to Pictland*; Woolf, *From Pictland to Alba, 789–1070*.

[28] Forsyth, *Language in Pictland*; and Forsyth, 'Literacy in Pictland'.

[29] Loyn, *The Vikings in Britain*; Downham, *Viking Kings of Britain and Ireland*; Edmonds, *Gaelic Influence in the Northumbrian Kingdom*.

[30] Brink, 'Who Were the Vikings?'.

out larger raids throughout the year and penetrate inland. By the end of the ninth century, the Vikings had formed permanent settlements, and would remain an identifiable presence on the island for the next two hundred years.

Finally, the Norman Conquest of England brought with it another significant linguistic influence on medieval Britain.[31] At the Battle of Hastings on 14 October 1066, Harold Godwinson, the last Anglo-Saxon king, was defeated and killed, after which the Norman challenger subsequently referred to as William the Conqueror was crowned king of England. The Conquest was perceived by contemporaries as a watershed moment that eventually ushered in a new king, language of rule, class of Norman nobility, and system of government. In addition to its political consequences, the Conquest also had a significant impact on the development of the English language. The daily language of commerce, government, and politics slowly became Norman French, which would eventually develop into its own dialect, known as Anglo-Norman or the French of England. Its grammatical, syntactical, and orthographic impact on Old English was substantial enough that the structure of the language itself changed, entering a new historical-linguistic phase known as Middle English, which is beyond the scope of this study.[32]

Many languages were spoken in early medieval Britain, but that alone does not make it multilingual. Multilingualism occurred when these languages interacted. How did such interactions take place? What does our evidence look like? Languages could be expressed orally (spoken), visually (sign language), or in written format (text).[33] Surviving evidence of multilingualism in an oral context is sparser because we are reliant on analysing surrounding languages to determine patterns of contact. Evidence of linguistic borrowing (when specific words are adopted from one language into another) and syntactic and grammatical influence (when contact between two languages changes grammatical patterns in the inflections of individual words or the structure of sentences) can help to tell us when two languages have been in frequent enough contact with one another that one altered something fundamental about another. Such linguistic changes can be seen by comparing languages within the same family. For example, if we compare a Germanic language like Old English with other Germanic languages on the continent and we find in Old English an expanded vocabulary, altered syntax, or changes in inflection patterns, we can conclude that Old English has changed over time. If we then compare Old English to the other languages its speakers had frequent historical contact with

---

[31] Williams, *The English and the Norman Conquest*; Thomas, *The Norman Conquest*; Faith, *The Moral Economy of the Countryside*.

[32] Ingham, *The Transmission of Anglo-Norman*.

[33] On medieval sign language, see Bruce, *Silence and Sign Language in Medieval Monasticism*.

and discover similar vocabulary and grammatical/syntactical patterns newly present in Old English, we can conclude that those languages had an influence on Old English. This type of linguistic influence worked both ways, and examining patterns of change can tell us what types of contact may have taken place between their speakers: an 'arriving' language new to a given region might bring technological vocabulary that would be adopted into an 'inhabitant' language at the same time as the 'arriving' language might also adopt terminology for native flora and fauna from the 'inhabitant' language. Placenames and personal names are another key source of evidence for oral contact across languages. When Old English placenames have Celtic rather than Germanic roots, we know that at least some individuals from these two language groups were in close enough contact with one another to exchange local information.[34] Similarly, personal names are a deliberate choice made by parents on behalf of their children reflective of their cultural surroundings. When a Welsh family gave their son an Old English name, an Anglo-Saxon family gave their son a French name, or the elements of an individual's name combined Old English and Cornish, we can deduce that they lived in a multilingual environment.

While individual moments of oral and visual communication were sometimes recorded in our source material, it is unsurprising that most of our surviving evidence for multilingualism in early medieval Britain is preserved in written form. Written material in early Britain was overwhelmingly set down using the Latin alphabet, with the additional occasional use of the runic (Germanic)[35] and ogham (Celtic)[36] alphabets discussed in Sections 1 and 3. This Element does not catalogue every multilingual interaction from pre-Norman Britain, but rather seeks to convey the range of languages, media, people, and events involved, via four sections' worth of thematic case studies. These case studies illustrate a range of scenarios: texts or manuscripts containing more than one language, individuals fluent in multiple tongues, political gatherings where several vernaculars were spoken, and documents translated from a known or lost original. There is naturally a good deal of overlap between the examples included, and another scholar could easily interpret them within a different organisational structure. I have chosen a thematic approach to illustrate the wide range of moments in early medieval Britain where multiple languages overlapped and interacted. Section 1 introduces the practicalities of multilingualism by selecting a few of the most memorable and interesting texts

---

[34] Jackson, *Language and History in Early Britain*; Padel, *Cornish Place-Name Elements*; Coates and Breeze, *Celtic Voices, English Places*.

[35] Barnes, *Runes*.

[36] Higgit, Forsyth, and Parsons, *Roman, Runes and Ogham*; Sims-Williams, *The Celtic Inscriptions of Britain*.

and manuscripts from across the early medieval period to study in depth. Section 2 focuses on multilingualism in a religious and intellectual context, considering especially the use of translated texts while the Anglo-Saxon kingdoms were in the process of conversion to Christianity. Section 3 explores the political nuances of multilingualism, paying close attention to oral translation and vernacular language acquisition. Section 4 delves into the economic and practical sides of multilingualism, focusing particularly on its impact in the lives of non-elites. The Conclusion wraps up by taking stock of where things stood on the eve of the Norman Conquest of England and looks briefly forward to the post-Norman period. This Element argues that early medieval Britain was not just a place where multiple languages were spoken: rather, it was a space where those languages interacted, and the culture and history that emerged were products of those interactions.

1 Manuscripts and Multilingual Texts

Our first section introduces the range of physical evidence available by selecting a few of the most memorable and interesting multilingual texts and manuscripts from across the early medieval period as lenses through which to comment on the particular cultural resonances of their multilingual elements. Other sections of this Element will explore multilingualism largely through the act of translation, in both written and oral contexts. Here, the focus is on texts, manuscripts, and objects such as inscribed stone monuments and artwork that incorporated two or more languages simultaneously and deliberately, underscoring the extent to which multilingualism was embraced across early medieval Britain as a means of artistic and intellectual expression.

We must first clarify some differences in the implications of multilingualism within texts versus within manuscripts. Multilingual texts are those in which an author has incorporated more than one language within the same work. This section will explore texts in which multiple languages have been deliberately combined, such as a cryptogram whose solution required a knowledge of both Latin and Greek; Old English charms which include lines of garbled Old Irish or Latin as incantations; macaronic poems combining Old English, Latin, and Greek into one text; and a Latin/Old-English glossary, an early form of dictionary. Such texts are clearly designed to showcase the fact that their authors knew multiple languages. Others may have been less intentional in nature, particularly those incorporating vernacular placenames into a Latin narrative, such as Asser's inclusion of Welsh placenames in his Latin biography of ninth-century West Saxon king Alfred the Great.[37] Multilingual manuscripts, on the other

---

[37] Keynes and Lapidge, *Alfred the Great.*

hand, contained several linguistic layers, not always written at the same time or by the same author, meaning that not every author or scribe who worked on these manuscripts had knowledge of more than one language. The layers of languages contained within these physical objects reveal the multilingual milieux in which they were produced, underscoring the range of linguistic knowledge circulating within the shared academic environment of early medieval Britain.

How did people in early medieval Britain learn a second language? As we will see below, many individuals acquired multiple vernacular languages during the course of their life experiences: a period of exile, a long voyage, a politically advantageous fosterage. For most second-language learners of Latin and other 'academic' languages like Greek, however, linguistic knowledge was taught via the same classroom tools and techniques that are still in use today. To explore this process in depth, we turn to our first case study: the text known as the Corpus Glossary (Cambridge, Corpus Christi College MS 144), produced in the early ninth century.[38] The Corpus Glossary contains 8,712 entries, making it the largest surviving alphabetical glossary from Anglo-Saxon England.[39] The bulk of this text is in Latin, but over 2,000 words are glossed in Old English in a Mercian dialect. The process through which the Corpus Glossary came to be was a complicated one. First, difficult words in individual manuscripts were glossed interlinearly (between lines of text) or marginally (in the blank margins of manuscript pages). These headwords, known as *lemmata*, and their explications were then stripped from their manuscript context and compiled into lists known as *glossae collectae*, which were copied again: first in batches by source text, and then rearranged alphabetically by the first letter of headwords. Finally, the Corpus Glossary scribe both recast many of the Latin explications in his sources into Old English and rearranged all the entries into AB alphabetical order (alphabetised by first and second letter) to produce the manuscript that remains today.[40]

The Corpus Glossary is composed of two discrete units, known as the First and Second Corpus Glossaries, that illustrate the strategies that scholars in early medieval Britain developed to learn, teach, and study texts in multiple languages. The First Corpus Glossary contains a list of largely Hebrew names from the Bible and Greek technical terms of grammar, metre, and rhetoric, with interpretations. The Second Corpus Glossary is a large collection of glossed *lemmata* in a mixture of Latin, Old English, and (mostly) transliterated Greek,

---

[38] Hessels, *An Eighth-Century Latin-Anglo-Saxon Glossary*; Lindsay, *The Corpus Glossary*; Lindsay, *The Corpus, Épinal, Erfurt and Leyden Glossaries*.

[39] Lendinara, *Anglo-Saxon Glosses and Glossaries*, 16.

[40] Lindsay, *The Corpus, Épinal, Erfurt and Leyden Glossaries*, 1–16; 36–8; 44–53.

rearranged in AB order. The incipits (openings) of these texts and the layout of the manuscript that contains them show that they were beautifully designed and spaced to complement one another. What can their form tell us about their function? The First Corpus Glossary, composed mostly of Hebrew names from the Bible and their interpretations, is much shorter, far more tightly focused, and easier to digest and navigate as an inclusive collection of material. Its focus is largely narrowed to a key subset of knowledge, Hebrew names and Greek terminology, which form 70 per cent of its included material.[41] A further 15 per cent of its contents takes the form of transliterated Greek terms of grammar, metre, and rhetoric, and their explications, drawn from a known grammatical glossary.[42] Several entries are trilingual, in the *tres linguae sacrae* (three sacred languages) of Hebrew, Greek and Latin. The community that designed and used the First Corpus Glossary did so for an audience that studied Hebrew names, Greek grammatical terms, and Old English encyclopaedic information regularly enough that a focused reference guide – in other words, a teaching tool – was deemed desirable.

The types of knowledge contained in both the First and Second Corpus Glossaries were valued by the community that produced them, but these documents were used for different reasons. The Second Corpus Glossary contains almost 9,000 entries in a blend of Latin, Old English, and transliterated Greek. It was designed for functionality: its AB order, clear spacing, and headwords for each section meant that it could function as a dictionary. Yet these entries were severed from the texts from which they were originally culled, which suggests an inherent value in the information in its own right. In other words, the Corpus Glossary functioned not only as a dictionary but also as an encyclopaedia. What types of knowledge could a reader have gained from a text like this? The Corpus Glossary incorporated material from a wide range of sources, including historical and classical works as well as Latin and Greek grammatical material. Even if the users of the Corpus Glossary did not have access to the complete texts from which these entries were originally stripped, a reader of this manuscript would still encounter an enormous amount of learning, in Latin, Greek, Hebrew, and Old English, from the classical and late antique worlds, and would need to be a fairly adept scholar already in order to successfully navigate it. The contents of the Corpus Glossary underscore the prevalence of multilingualism in the scholarly milieu of early medieval Britain,

---

[41] Lapidge, 'The School of Theodore and Hadrian'; Pheifer, 'Early Anglo-Saxon Glossaries and the School of Canterbury'.

[42] Lendinara, *Anglo-Saxon Glosses and Glossaries*, 18; glossary ed. Gneuss, 'A Grammarian's Greek-Latin Glossary in Anglo-Saxon England'.

as well as some strategies adopted by scholars to teach and learn multiple academic languages.

Multiple languages could be combined within texts in very practical ways. In Section 3, we will consider some charters which blend Latin legal formulae with Old English boundary clauses. Yet it would be narrow-minded to view the multilingualism of these texts as purely utilitarian. They also suggest the belief that some languages were a more fitting reflection of certain ideas than others. A beautiful illustration of this concept can be found in the Franks Casket (Figure 1), an early eighth-century carved whalebone box, most of which is now owned by the British Museum.[43] Its five decorative panels contain a range of scenes representing an intriguing mixture of Germanic, classical, and biblical imagery. The carved scenes on the Franks Casket are also accompanied by textual inscriptions that function as captions to these images. The textual inscriptions are in a mixture of Old English and Latin, and the alphabets used to write these languages are in turn a mixture of the Latin and runic alphabets. Most of the Franks Casket's inscriptions are in runic Old English, but it is fascinating to see that the Latin language and alphabet are used only to describe a classical scene: the taking of Jerusalem by the Roman emperor Titus during

Figure 1 The Franks Casket, left panel. Image from Wikimedia Commons, public domain.

---

[43] The right-hand panel is in the Museo Nazionale del Bargello, Florence, Italy.

the First Jewish-Roman War. The Franks Casket combines text and image, the Old English and Latin languages, and the runic and Latin alphabets together into one thoughtfully produced object. Its use of the Latin language and alphabet only on a panel depicting a classical scene also suggests that particular languages were perceived to be more closely associated with certain ideas than others.

The Franks Casket was clearly designed as a prestige object, as were many other multilingual texts in early medieval Britain. One of the most obvious cases in which multilingualism was used to make a public statement was the creation of stone monuments inscribed in both Latin in the Latin alphabet and Gaelic in the ogham alphabet.[44] These monuments commemorated wealthy and influential individuals and were erected at prominent sites on the landscape that would have been visible to passers-by. The use of two languages in these inscriptions speaks to the continued knowledge of both by some individuals in post-Roman Britain and implies an audience who was at least able to distinguish them, if not read one or both.[45]

Scholars also delighted in showing off their knowledge of multiple languages by crafting literary works whose interpretation required multilingual skill. One such genre of works are macaronic poems, which combined Old English, Latin, and occasionally Greek together in one text. For instance, most of the poem known as *The Phoenix* is written in Old English, but its author also includes eleven lines of macaronic verse in which the first half of every line is in Old English, and the second half of the line is in Latin, as follows:

Hafað us alyfed	lucis auctor
þæt we motun her	merueri
goddædum begietan	gaudia in celo
þær we motum	maxima regna
secan ond gesittan	sedibus altis
lifgan in lisse	lucis et pacis
agan eardinga	alma letitie
brucan blæddaga	blandem et mittem
geseon sigora frean	sine fine
ond him lof singan	laude perenne
eadge mid englum.	Alleluia.

---

[44] Charles-Edwards, *Wales and the Britons*, 75–173; Redknap and Lewis, *A Corpus of Early Medieval Inscribed Stones and Stone Sculptures in Wales*, vol. 1 and Edwards, *A Corpus of Early Medieval Inscribed Stones and Stone Sculptures in Wales*, vol. 2 and vol. 3.

[45] Edwards, 'Material Evidence and Identity'.

(The author of light has granted to us that we are able to merit and to achieve by good deeds here joys in heaven; there we might seek the greatest kingdoms and take a seat upon the high thrones, to live in the grace of light and of peace, to own abodes of gracious rejoicing, to enjoy happy days, to see the lord of victories, pleasant and mild, without end, and to sing praise to him by means of perpetual adulation, blissfully among the angels. Alleluia.)[46]

Another macaronic poem, known as *Aldhelm*, goes a step further and combines Old English, Latin, and Greek into one (imperfect) text. (As Fred C. Robinson comments, 'the poet's ambition to compose a poem in three languages at once exceeded his talents'.)[47] Macaronic poems like these required a knowledge of multiple languages for both their composition and their interpretation, and such works therefore served to show off their authors' erudition at the same time as reading them correctly would have served as a litmus test for the education of a reader. We will return to the idea of linguistic skill as a shibboleth for intelligence in the case of the Bamberg cryptogram below.

Our discussion thus far has focused on multilingual texts containing Old English alongside Latin, Greek, or Hebrew: that is, languages which were learned and taught in an academic or ecclesiastical milieu. But these were not the only varieties of multilingual texts that existed in early medieval Britain, nor were they restricted to elites. An insight into the role that multilingualism may have played within a broader proportion of the medieval population, as within an oral as opposed to a purely written context, can be found in a group of texts known as the Old English charms. These brief texts, written in both poetry and prose, contained incantations whose utterance or performance was intended to bring about some real-world effect: a cure for illness, the rejuvenation of unproductive land, the return of stolen cattle. The charms appear alongside medical recipes in manuscripts that compiled hundreds of these texts together and were clearly also considered to be medicinal in nature by their medieval authors and practitioners. Modern scholars have distinguished a 'charm' from a 'recipe' by their additional incantations: words or phrases intended to be spoken aloud in order for the charm to work. Some charms also contained a set of actions to be performed while the incantations were spoken. The Old English charms have long fascinated scholars due to their mixture of pagan and Christian elements, and these brief texts represent one of the few written insights we possess into the practical religious, medicinal, and folk beliefs of medieval non-elites.[48]

---

[46] *The Phoenix*, ll. 667–77; ed. and trans. Cain, 'Old English Macaronic Verses', 277–8.

[47] Robinson, 'Two Old English Poems', 197.

[48] Jolly, *Popular Religion in Late Saxon England*.

The Old English charms also offer a rare window into multilingualism amongst a wider segment of the population of early medieval Britain, because their base text is Old English but their incantations are often in garbled forms of other languages, including Latin and Old Irish.[49] As Tiffany Beechy argues: 'the point is the form, not the meaning'.[50] Studies of the Old English charms largely agree that the high degree to which their multilingual components have been garbled was part of their perceived efficacy. To quote Beechy again: 'the "Holy Salve" charm prescribes "Acre arcre arnem nona ærnem beoðor ærnem nidren acrun cunað ele harassan fidine" . . . there is no meaning to translate; the language is perfectly opaque'.[51] The indecipherability of the charms' multilingual elements effects their potency. But when considering these texts as part of the broader multilingual landscape of early medieval Britain, we can also draw a few additional conclusions. First of all, a wider proportion of the population would have encountered multiple languages, however garbled, via texts like these charms than would have read material like the Corpus Glossary or the *Phoenix*. Secondly, even though the Latin or Old Irish incantations in the charms are garbled, the fact that these languages are still recognisable means that the people who initially composed the charms encountered enough Latin or Old Irish to include it in their texts. Thirdly, even in their garbled form, the key fact remains that multiple languages were believed to be useful: in this case as incantations with the power to ward off disease. And finally, as in the cases of the Latin/Old English charters and the Franks Casket discussed above, in these charms we again can witness the perception that certain languages were understood to be a better fit for certain contexts than others. In this case, Old English was used to narrate the charms' practical 'instructions' and a non-native language to perform their spoken incantations.

For our final textual case study, we return to an intellectual milieu and an item that illustrates the political nuances of multilingualism as a marker of learning, as well as the playfulness that it could inspire. The brief text known as the Bamberg Cryptogram was written in the ninth century by an Irish scholar named Dubthach mac Máel-Tuile who was residing in Britain at the court of Welsh king Merfyn Frych. The cryptogram is a puzzle written in both Latin and Greek letters whose solution requires 'the substitution of Greek letters for Latin in accordance with a fixed table'.[52] Its text reads, 'IB E IZ IB E IΓ. IZ E KA. Γ IΔ IΓ Γ H IΓ. IH A IA K IΘ E IB', the solution of which is 'Mermen rex Conchn salutem', that is, 'King Merfyn greets Cyngen' (a line from a letter to Cyngen ap

[49] Meroney, 'Irish in the Old English Charms'.   [50] Beechy, *Poetics of Old English*, 86.
[51] Beechy, *Poetics of Old English*, 86.
[52] Chadwick, 'Early Culture and Learning in North Wales', 95.

Cadell ap Brochfael, Merfyn Frych's brother-in-law).[53] The text of the crypto-gram survives in two manuscripts, one of which embeds it in a letter containing both a detailed explanation of the puzzle's solution as well as some fascinating glimpses into the political, intellectual, and linguistic relationships that extended across early medieval Britain and Ireland.

As the beginning of this letter explains:

> This is an inscription that Dubthach in the fortress of Merfin king of the Britons sent out for testing wise Scots [i.e. 'Irishmen'], supposing himself to be most excellent of all Scots and Britons, thinking, understand, that none of the learned men of the Scots-born – how much more of the Britons – in the presence of Merfin the king could read through and understand this writing. But with us, Caunchobrach, Fergus and Dominnach and Suadbar, investigating the same inscription, with God supporting, by means of the computus [lit. 'calendrical book'] and the little book of the alphabet of the Greeks, that writing did not lie hidden.[54]

As the letter's author, Suadbar, makes clear, both the cryptogram and the letter detailing its solution use multilingualism to show off: linguistic skill is treated as a proxy for intelligence in a contest of academic one-upmanship. This is a contest, Suadbar's letter makes clear, that he believes he has won. His text concludes by pointing out a spelling error in the puzzle itself: 'Here you err, Dubthach, in your little notes, writing H for Θ or for E or for a note of aspiration, which according to the Brittonic language does not sound well in that position.'[55] Dubthach's cryptogram was designed to display his own knowledge of Latin and Greek and to test that of others, but Suadbar's solution implies that he is the superior scholar by pointing out flaws in Dubthach's Welsh! Bearing in mind that both Dubthach and Suadbar were Irish scholars, the Bamberg Cryptogram, in actuality, reflects the quadrilingual intellectual milieu through which they moved.

Suadbar's letter takes the form of a detailed explication of the cryptogram's solution, memorably concluding

> not as if to you being ignorant are we sending this little exposition, but we humbly request that this explanation to our Scots-born brothers, ignorant and more simple, wishing to ship across the British sea, through your well-wishing charity you might insinuate, lest by chance in the presence of Merfin the glorious king of the Britons, not understanding that inscription, they might blush.[56]

As Nora K. Chadwick commented: 'In other words he asks Colgu to make sure that his countrymen may memorise the crib before visiting Mermin's court,

---

[53] Howlett, 'Two Irish Jokes', 235, 239, and 244.   [54] Howlett, 'Two Irish Jokes', 238–9.
[55] Howlett, 'Two Irish Jokes', 240.   [56] Howlett, 'Two Irish Jokes', 240.

where it will be put to them as an intelligence test. What a delightful bit of patriotic cheating!'.[57]

While it is highly unlikely that travelling scholars were regularly required to solve cryptograms in order to gain entrance to the courts they visited, Suadbar's 'delightful bit of patriotic cheating' serves as a very literal illustration of the degree to which knowledge of multiple languages functioned as a shibboleth for both natural intelligence and level of education in the shared intellectual milieu of early medieval Britain and Ireland. At the same time, the context of the Bamberg Cryptogram's composition and solution reminds us of the frequency of movement between the two islands and of Suadbar's closing remarks that early medieval scholars paid just as much attention to the grammatical accuracy of vernacular languages as they did to Latin and Greek.

The Bamberg Cryptogram was a product of the multilingual intellectual community that spanned across Britain, Ireland, and the continent in the early medieval period. Further evidence of the vibrancy of this intellectual milieu can be seen in multilingual manuscripts. Manuscripts are compilations which contain layers of texts, sometimes produced at different places and times and by different authors. While they do not always demonstrate that a single author knew more than one language in the way that multilingual texts do, these manuscripts do reflect the reality that the *scriptoria* which produced them were multilingual institutions and that these manuscripts were written, read, and annotated by scholars from a range of linguistic backgrounds. The first multilingual manuscript we will consider, Cambridge University Library MS Ff.4.42, is known as the *Cambridge Juvencus* (Figure 2) because the primary text it contains is a tenth-century copy of a work by the poet of that name.[58] The *Cambridge Juvencus*, however, was continuously worked and reworked by a number of different scholars from a range of linguistic backgrounds over the course of the late ninth and tenth centuries, most of whom left traces of their presence on its pages. In addition to its main text, a copy of a Latin work by Juvencus, this manuscript is heavily annotated, with marginal and interlinear glosses and brief compositions in Latin, Old Welsh, and Old Irish.

Palaeographical and codicological evidence suggest that the manuscript was produced in Wales, 'making it an exceptional survival'.[59] The *Cambridge Juvencus* offers us a rare window through which to glimpse the intellectual activities that took place within this region of early medieval Britain, and what this manuscript shows us is the range of linguistic backgrounds that the scholars who worked on this manuscript possessed. For instance, the main scribe of the

---

[57] Chadwick, 'Early Culture and Learning in North Wales', 96.

[58] The following information on the *Cambridge Juvencus* is drawn from Williams, 'Cambridge Juvencus', where a digital facsimile of the manuscript can also be viewed.

[59] Williams, 'Cambridge Juvencus'.

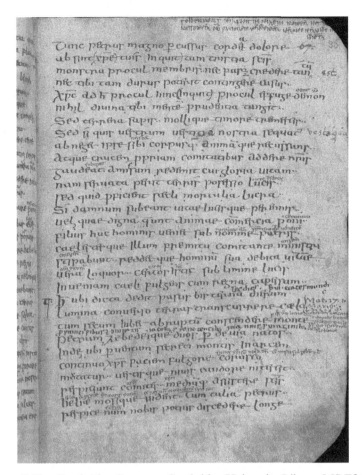

Figure 2 The *Cambridge Juvencus*, Cambridge University Library MS Ff.4.42, fol. 36r, showing a multilingual cryptogram and interlinear and marginal glossing. Reproduced by kind permission of the Syndics of Cambridge University Library.

Cambridge Juvencus signed his name, itself another rarity, as Núadu, in a colophon reading *Araut dinuadu*, 'A prayer for Núadu'. This colophon was written in Old Welsh, but its structure 'follows an Irish formula', and Núadu itself is an Irish name, together suggesting 'evidence for an Irish scribe working in Wales during the tenth century':[60] evidence which tallies very well with the intellectual milieu in which the Bamberg Cryptogram was produced.

Moreover, thirteen additional scribes annotated the *Cambridge Juvencus* in some way after Núadu had copied the initial text, and most of these annotations reflect multilingualism in some way. For example, fol. 36r contains a cryptogram whose solution relies on the same Latin/Greek key as that of the

---

[60] Williams, 'Cambridge Juvencus'.

Bamberg Cryptogram, which we know to have been composed by an Irish scholar, but produces the Welsh name 'Cymelliauc'. Again, we find evidence for a quadrilingual intellectual environment in the *scriptorium* which produced the *Cambridge Juvencus*. As to which *scriptorium* that was, as Myriah Williams has argued, 'a location near the border between Wales and England may be supported by an error in a gloss made by Scribe G on fol. 20r, where the third letter p in the Old Welsh "papep bi" must have been a þ representing *th* in the exemplar from which the scribe was copying'; 'the Anglo-Saxon letter form þ' thus suggesting an exemplar produced 'somewhere near or in England'.[61] Elsewhere in the manuscript, Scribe C's annotations include Welsh verse and Latin hexameters, one of which includes the Irish name Féthgna, in addition to 'errors in the Old Welsh verses that may indicate he was in fact an Irish speaker'.[62] On the whole, then, the *Cambridge Juvencus* reveals the existence of a vibrant intellectual community in early medieval Wales, which drew to itself scholars whose linguistic backgrounds encompassed Latin, Old Welsh, Old Irish, and Old English.

The multilingual intellectual milieu of early medieval Britain can be seen not only in the range of native languages that its scholars spoke, but also in the way that centres of manuscript production sought out and compiled multilingual material. This process is beautifully illustrated by the manuscript known as *St Dunstan's Classbook* (Oxford, Bodleian Library, MS Auct. F. 4. 32) (Figure 3).[63] *St Dunstan's Classbook* is a composite manuscript assembled in four distinct parts, three of which bear the hand of the Anglo-Saxon abbot and saint Dunstan of Glastonbury, whence it derives its title. It is believed that St Dunstan brought the individual booklets of his *Classbook* together at Glastonbury Abbey sometime before he became Archbishop of Canterbury in 960. The manuscript also draws its name from a famous frontispiece on folio 1r, which depicts a monk, identified as Dunstan in a hexameter couplet, prostrating himself in front of Christ. From a multilingual perspective, *St Dunstan's Classbook* is valuable for both the linguistic range of its primary texts and its wealth of glossed material. Part I of the manuscript (fols. 1–9) contains a fragmentary grammatical treatise by Eutyches on the conjugation of Latin verbs, copied in the mid-ninth century. The text includes a number of interlinear and marginal glosses in Latin and Old Breton, suggesting that this part of the manuscript may originally have been produced in Brittany. Part II (fols. 10–18) is an Old English homily on the invention of the cross, in an Anglo-Saxon script

[61] Williams, 'Cambridge Juvencus'.   [62] Williams, 'Cambridge Juvencus'.

[63] Hunt, *Saint Dunstan's Classbook from Glastonbury*. Digital facsimile available at http://image
.ox.ac.uk/show?collection=bodleian&manuscript=msauctf432 and online manuscript descriptions: Da Rold, 'Classbook of St. Dunstan' and Hayward, 'St Dunstan's Classbook'.

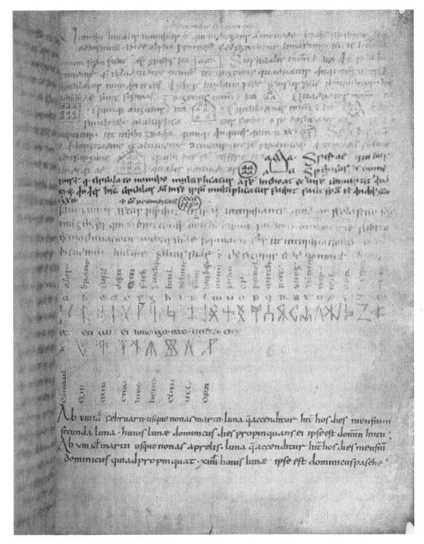

Figure 3 *St Dunstan's Classbook*, Oxford, Bodleian Library, MS Auct. F. 4. 32, fol. 20r, showing the 'alphabet of Nemnivus'. Image from Wikimedia Commons, public domain.

dating to the eleventh century. Part III (fols. 19–36) is known as the *Liber Commonei*, the 'book of Commoneus', as a colophon states that the text was written upon his request. The *Liber Commonei* was produced in Wales during the first half of the ninth century and contains a variety of computistical and liturgical texts. Most of its main texts are in Latin and Greek, and are heavily glossed, including glosses in Old Welsh. Significant Irish intellectual influence underlies this text's computistical material, and a curious text known as the 'alphabet of Nemnivus' (fol. 20r) – which offers a Welsh version of a runic alphabet – was modelled on either the Old English *futhorc*, the Old Irish *ogham* alphabet, or some combination of the two.[64] Finally, Part IV (fols. 37–47) contains a copy of book one of Ovid's *Ars Amatoria* ('The Art of Love') which dates to the late ninth or early tenth century and includes many interlinear glosses in Latin and Old Welsh.[65]

An extraordinarily impressive range of languages, scribal hands, and intellectual traditions came together to produce the components of *St Dunstan's Classbook*. Two of its booklets were written in ninth-century Wales; a third in ninth-century Wales or Brittany; and the fourth in Anglo-Saxon England. Together, they incorporate material in Latin, Greek, Old English, Old Breton, and Old Welsh, with additional Irish influence underlying the computistical material in the *Liber Commonei* and the 'alphabet of Nemnivus'. Moreover, all of this material was of interest to the Anglo-Saxon saint and scholar Dunstan, who compiled these texts together by the mid-tenth century. Dunstan's location at Glastonbury Abbey was likely to have been a significant factor in the *Classbook*'s multilingual nature. There were reports of an 'Irish school' at Glastonbury 'by the tenth century at the latest', and 'St Dunstan's earliest biographer' 'relates that Dunstan himself studied with the Irish at Glastonbury'.[66] Multilingual intellectual influence shaped the creation of *St Dunstan's Classbook*, and as its compiler's annotations show, the composite manuscript was studied and used as a text in its own right. In tenth-century Glastonbury, we find an intellectual environment that valued and perpetuated multilingualism in the manuscripts it chose to acquire and learn from.

Glossed manuscripts are also crucial to our understanding of multilingualism in early medieval Britain because they preserve evidence of intellectual activity in regions from which few independent texts survive. We have already seen the value of glossed manuscripts in preserving otherwise rare specimens of Old Welsh, and they are perhaps even more important for our knowledge of Cornish. The known corpus of Cornish in the early medieval period is comprised solely of words found in glossed manuscripts and vocabulary lists: no complete sentence of Cornish survives. The earliest independent narrative texts, known collectively as the *Ordinalia*, are a group of three Middle Cornish mystery plays that date to the late fourteenth century. Thus, we are fortunate that two multilingual manuscripts from early medieval Britain survive to shed light not only on this period of the Cornish language, but also on the degree to which early

---

[64] Russell, 'Between Ogam and Runes'.   [65] Russell, *Reading Ovid in Medieval Wales*.
[66] Carley, 'Two Pre-conquest Manuscripts from Glastonbury Abbey', 197.

medieval Cornwall belonged to the same multilingual insular intellectual milieu that we have already studied. The first is known as *De raris fabulis* ('some other uncommon tales'; Oxford, Bodleian Library, MS. Bodley 572 [SC 2026], fols. 41v-47r) (Figure 4). Its base text is a series of schoolroom exercises for learning Latin, which takes the form of a dialogue between pupil and teacher. *De raris fabulis* also contains almost 200 glosses, both interlinear and embedded within the text, in Latin, Old Cornish, Old Welsh, and Old English. Scott Gwara has argued that this manuscript was originally produced in Cornwall,[67] further underscoring the range of linguistic activity that shaped the intellectual landscape of early medieval Britain. While our surviving corpora of Old Welsh and Old Cornish are much smaller than those of Old English and Old Irish, manuscripts like *De raris fabulis* reflect the vibrancy of these languages as part of the insular intellectual community.

Our final multilingual manuscript takes a slightly different form, but is no less significant for our understanding of both early Cornish and multilingualism more broadly. The text known as the *Bodmin Manumissions* (London, British Library, Additional MS. 9381) is a Latin gospel-book whose margins were used to record about fifty manumissions (freeings) of slaves in Cornwall from the mid-tenth century to about 1100.[68] The base text of the gospel-book itself was produced in Brittany in the late ninth century, thus underscoring, like *St Dunstan's Classbook*, the close intellectual ties between Britain and the continent during the early medieval period. Once the gospel-book was brought to Cornwall, 'within half a century of being written',[69] it arrived at the church of St Petrock, where it was used to record the names of participants and witnesses to ceremonies of manumission. The exact location where these ceremonies took place is unknown, because St Petrock's church moved from Padstow to Bodmin at some point during the period when the manumissions were recorded, possibly in response to Viking attacks.[70]

The multilingualism of the *Bodmin Manumissions* is multifaceted. First of all, its manumissions are recorded in a mixture of Latin and Old English. Secondly, the names of those participating in and witnessing the manumission ceremonies span a wide linguistic range: not just Cornish and Old English, but also Scandinavian and Irish. As Oliver Padel writes, the *Bodmin Manumissions* 'vividly illustrates how Cornwall's peninsular and maritime nature has rendered it constantly open to immigrants who have settled and become native'.[71] The *Bodmin Manumissions* also offer us rare insight into the practical realities of

---

[67] Gwara, 'Understanding *De raris fabulis*'; Gwara, '*De raris fabulis*'.
[68] Padel, 'The Bodmin Manumissions'; Insley, 'Languages of Boundaries'.
[69] Padel, 'The Bodmin Manumissions', 8.   [70] Padel, 'The Bodmin Manumissions', 6.
[71] Padel, 'The Bodmin Manumissions', 14, with Appendix on personal names 32–3.

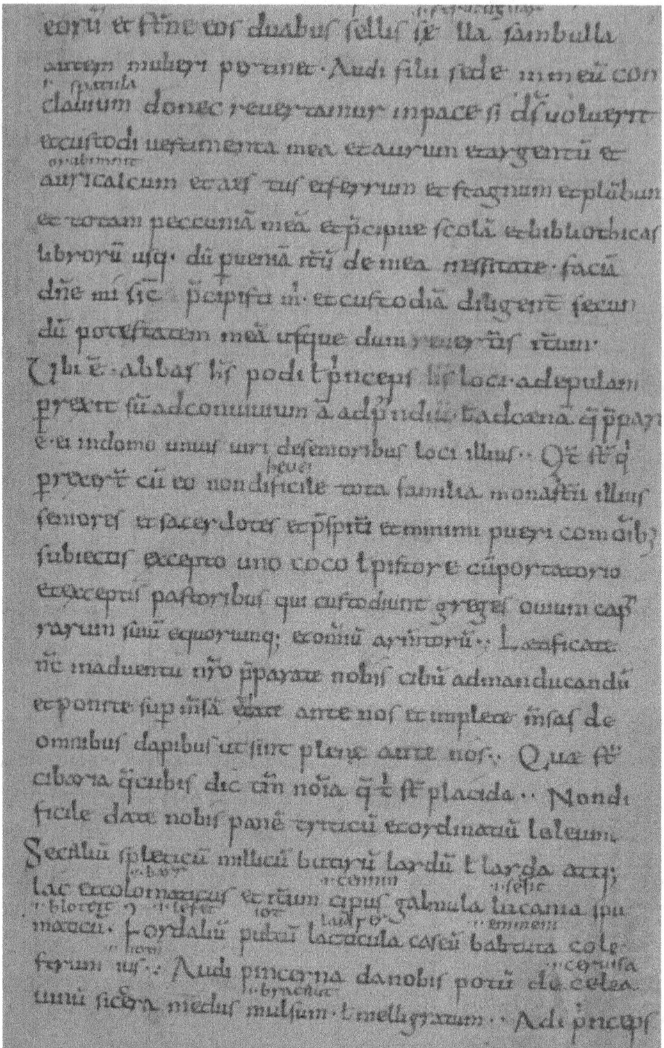

Figure 4 *De raris fabulis*, Oxford, Bodleian Library, MS. Bodley 572 [SC 2026], fols. 41v–47r, fol. 42r, showing interlinear glossing. Image from Wikimedia Commons, public domain.

multilingualism at the very lowest social strata. The entries encompass four groups of people: 'the slaves freed, the owners freeing them, the people for whose souls the action was done (often the owners themselves), and the witnesses'.[72] In these manumissions, we can see the real-world implications of multilingualism on early medieval Cornish and Anglo-Saxon society. Most

---

[72] Padel, 'The Bodmin Manumissions', 8.

of the names in the *Bodmin Manumissions* are Cornish, but the manumissions are recorded in Latin or Old English, reminding us that Cornish-speakers would have witnessed or participated in important legal ceremonies conducted in a language that was not their native tongue. Some of the recorded names are also a hybrid blend of Cornish and Old English elements, reflecting the reality that intermarriage created multilingual communities.[73] The *Bodmin Manumissions* serves as a key reminder of the many communities across early medieval Britain where multilingualism was a lived reality.

2 Saints and Scholars

The texts and manuscripts surveyed in Section 1 illustrate the broad range of multilingual media produced in early medieval Britain. Written evidence for the earliest multilingual milieu in post-Roman Britain survives but must be compiled from a variety of sources. We know that Latin survived alongside the vernacular British language after the Roman departure. The sixth-century British author Gildas's *De excidio et conquestu Britanniae*, the earliest surviving text from post-Roman Britain, testifies to the continued preservation of Latin as a written language,[74] and Peter Schrijver and others have argued that it also survived as a spoken language outside the church in southern Britain.[75] The dual Latin and Gaelic inscribed stone monuments noted in Section 1 also testify to the continued knowledge of Latin in post-Roman Britain. Some of these monuments are roughly contemporary with Gildas, providing additional evidence for continued knowledge of Latin as well as crucial information about the language's development: unlike texts preserved in later manuscripts, the form of the language cannot be updated on stone carvings.[76] This continued use of Latin after the departure of the Romans reminds us of its centrality within an ecclesiastical setting, where the vast majority of early medieval texts and manuscripts were produced. This section therefore surveys multilingualism within the overlapping religious and intellectual spheres, thinking particularly about the key role that textual translations played in the conversion of the Anglo-Saxon kingdoms to Christianity and the works that Christian communities in early Britain produced.

One of the earliest and most important recorded episodes of Anglo-Saxon history, their conversion to Christianity at the hands of Roman missionaries, has multilingualism at its heart. The linchpin event in Bede's *Historia Ecclesiastica*

---

[73] Padel, 'The Bodmin Manumissions', 10.
[74] Winterbottom, *Gildas*; Lapidge and Dumville, *Gildas: New Approaches*.
[75] Schrijver, 'What Britons Spoke around 400 AD'.
[76] Charles-Edwards, *Wales and the Britons*, 75–173 and Edwards, 'Material Evidence and Identity'.

gentis Anglorum – which, as its title suggests, relates the narrative of the Anglo-Saxons' transition from paganism to Christianity – was the conversion mission sent by Pope Gregory the Great and carried out by Augustine of Canterbury in 597. Bede's narrative is a simple one: Augustine sailed from the continent to the Isle of Thanet, where he began preaching and converted Æthelberht, king of Kent. Other kings and kingdoms soon followed, and all of the Anglo-Saxon kingdoms were nominally converted to Christianity by the end of the seventh century. But how did this conversion take place on a practical level? When the Gregorian mission and events surrounding it are examined in detail, moments of multilingualism emerge as crucial factors. When Augustine and his companions sailed to Kent, 'they had acquired interpreters from the Frankish race according to the command of Pope St. Gregory',[77] and began the conversion mission by writing to Æthelberht through these interpreters – presumably in Old English? – and announcing their intentions. After Augustine and his companions were warmly received by Æthelberht, Bede lets slip the detail that their path had been paved by a prior 'missionary' of sorts. He writes, 'some knowledge about the Christian religion had already reached him [Æthelberht] because he had a Christian wife of the Frankish royal family whose name was Bertha. He had received her from her parents on condition that she be allowed to practise her faith and religion unhindered, with a bishop named Liudhard whom they had provided for her to support her faith'.[78] The intersection of multilingualism and marriage will be discussed further in Section 3, but the Gregorian mission to convert the Anglo-Saxons likely owed its success to the multilingual milieu in which it was undertaken: interpreters from the Frankish kingdom who could speak Old English, as well as prior exposure to Latin (and Christianity) via the retinue of Æthelberht's Frankish wife Bertha. Even in the pre-conversion period, we find evidence of multilingualism and open channels of communication between the continent and Anglo-Saxon England, as well as between the latter and the Celtic-speaking world.

More detailed episodes elsewhere in the *Historia Ecclesiastica* help us understand how interactions such as these would have taken place on a practical level. Bede's narrative makes clear the substantial Irish influence in Northumbria and on the early Anglo-Saxon church,[79] a key moment of which was the arrival of Irish bishop Aidan, founder of the prominent monastic centre of Lindisfarne, at the behest of Northumbrian king Oswald. Bede relates that 'it was indeed a beautiful sight when the bishop was preaching the gospel, to see

---

[77] Colgrave and Mynors, *Bede's Ecclesiastical History of the English People*, i.25, 73.

[78] Colgrave and Mynors, *Bede's Ecclesiastical History of the English People*, i.25, 73–5.

[79] See McCann, *The Irish in the 'Historia Ecclesiastica Gentis Anglorum'* and Ireland, *The Gaelic Background of Old English Poetry before Bede.*

the king acting as interpreter of the heavenly word for his ealdormen and thegns, for the bishop was not completely at home in the English tongue, while the king had gained a perfect knowledge of Irish during the long period of his exile'.[80] The relationship between exile and multilingualism will be discussed further in Section 3, but the details of Aidan's and Oswald's relationship illustrate some of the ways in which influential religious figures in early medieval Britain not only practically acquired multilingual skills thanks to their life experiences, but also embraced them as a tool that would aid in the all-important programme of conversion to Christianity. Interpreters were a significant part of the Christian landscape of early medieval Britain. At the Synod of Whitby, where the 'correct' method of calculating the date of Easter was hotly debated, Bede's account makes a point of repeatedly highlighting the key role of interpreters. He writes that among the participants was 'Bishop Cedd, who, as has been mentioned, had been consecrated long before by the Irish and who acted as a most careful interpreter for both parties at the council' and that during the Synod, Agilbert stated: 'I request that my disciple, the priest Wilfrid, may speak on my behalf, for we are both in agreement with the other followers of our church tradition who are here present; and he can explain our views in the English tongue better and more clearly than I can through an interpreter'.[81]

Multilingualism also stood at the heart of early medieval Britain's intellectual landscape. This overlapped almost completely with its ecclesiastical landscape because Christianity brought with it literacy and the Latin alphabet. The multilingual scope of intellectual tradition can be witnessed in the famous 'Nennian preface' to the early ninth-century British Latin text known as the *Historia Brittonum*,[82] which in part reads, 'I have therefore made a heap of all that I have found, both from the Annals of the Romans and from the Chronicles of the Holy Fathers, and from the writings of the Irish and the English, and out of the tradition of our elders'.[83] While scholars no longer take this statement at face value, recognising the agency of medieval authors in shaping their texts to suit their own political agendas,[84] it still sheds valuable light on the intellectual landscape of early medieval Britain as one which contained source material from multiple linguistic traditions.[85] Throughout the text of the *Historia Brittonum*, its author matter-of-factly comments on his access to these sources:

---

[80] Colgrave and Mynors, *Bede's Ecclesiastical History of the English People*, iii.3, 220–1.
[81] Colgrave and Mynors, *Bede's Ecclesiastical History of the English People*, iii.25, 299 and 301.
[82] Guy, 'The Origins of the Compilation of Welsh Historical Texts in Harley 3859'; Russell, 'Two Notes on *Historia Brittonum*'.
[83] Morris, *Nennius*, 50 and 9.
[84] Dumville, 'Sub-Roman Britain: History and Legend' and 'The Historical Value of the *Historia Brittonum*'.
[85] Thomas, *History and Identity in Early Medieval Wales*, Ch. 3, 'Origin Legends I: The Britons'.

for example, at one point he notes, 'if anyone wants to know when Ireland was inhabited and when it was deserted, this is what the Irish scholars have told me'.[86]

Multilingualism continued to be a significant part of the intellectual and religious landscape of early medieval Britain after the conversion of the Anglo-Saxons. One significant early multilingual text is the vernacular Old English poem known as *Cædmon's Hymn*, first described in Bede's *Historia Ecclesiastica*. The events surrounding the purported composition of the poem took place during the late seventh century, and *Cædmon's Hymn* has a claim to being the oldest surviving datable poem in Old English. In the *Historia Ecclesiastica*, Bede describes how Cædmon, a lay cowherd at the monastery of Whitby, left a feast in embarrassment that he had no skill in composing poetry. When he fell asleep later that night, he had a dream and was divinely inspired to compose and recite Christian poetry, a skill he retained upon awaking. Bede preserves a translation of *Cædmon's Hymn*, the supposed first and only surviving one of Cædmon's poems, into Latin.[87] However, twenty-one medieval manuscripts of Bede's *Historia Ecclesiastica* also preserve Old English versions of this poem in several different dialects.[88] The preservation of the *Cædmon's Hymn* episode in Bede's Latin *Historia Ecclesiastica* along-side its Old English variants in the margins underscores the importance of both languages to early Anglo-Saxon Christian culture.

Bede translated a key vernacular religious text into Latin within the narrative of the *Historia Ecclesiastica*, but when it came to the role of multilingualism in early Anglo-Saxon Christianity, translation from Latin to the vernacular was equally crucial in the promotion of Christian texts to as wide an audience as possible. For instance, the *Historia Ecclesiastica* itself was not only widely cited in subsequent centuries,[89] it was also translated into the vernacular languages of Old English and Middle Irish.[90] Alfred the Great famously promoted a programme of learning during his reign, including the translation of major Latin works of both a religious and secular nature. The texts which were produced by the Alfredian translation programme underscore the range of topics which early medieval scholars saw value in reproducing in the vernacular: Old English translations of the *Pastoral Care* (Pope Gregory the Great's

---

[86] Morris, *Nennius*, 62 and 21.

[87] Colgrave and Mynors, *Bede's Ecclesiastical History of the English People*, iv.24, 416–17.

[88] O'Donnell, *Cædmon's Hymn*.

[89] Gransden, 'Bede's Reputation as an Historian in Medieval England'.

[90] Old English: Rowley, *The Old English Version of Bede's Historia Ecclesiastica*; Old Irish: Bergin, 'A Middle-Irish Fragment of Bede's Ecclesiastical History'; Ní Chatháin, 'Bede's Ecclesiastical History in Irish'; Ní Mhaonaigh, 'The Earliest Writing from Ireland, Scotland and Wales'.

Cura Pastoralis), the Old English *Boethius* (Boethius's *Consolation of Philosophy*), the Old English *Soliloquies* (St Augustine's *Soliloquies*), the Old English *Psalms* (the first fifty psalms), the Old English version of Gregory the Great's *Dialogues*, the Old English *Orosius* (Paulus Orosius's *Historiae adversus paganos*), and the Old English version of Bede's *Historia Ecclesiastica*.

Medieval authors and translators shared a widespread understanding that the process of translation was, in the words of Alfred the Great (himself translating a well-known Latin phrase into the vernacular), 'hwilum word be worde, hwilum andgit of andgite' (sometimes word for word; sometimes sense for sense).[91] Many religious texts were translated word-for-word from Latin into Old English. Examples include glossed texts, such as the *Vespasian Psalter*; prose texts, such as Bede's now-lost Old English translation of the Gospel of John or the later Old English *Life of St Mary of Egypt*; and poetic texts, such as the translation of Lacantius's *Carmen de ave Phoenice* into the Old English allegorical poem known as *The Phoenix*. Many scholars have observed that early medieval translations of Latin religious material into vernacular languages were just as often adaptations – that is, 'sense-for-sense' – as they were direct translations.[92] Such texts adhered to the central message of the works they translated, but added or revised details in order to adopt them more broadly to Anglo-Saxon culture. Examples of such adaptations include numerous Old English poems, such as *Christ and Satan*, *Andreas*, *Guthlac A*, and *Elene*, as well as prose translations such as Ælfric of Eynsham's *Lives of Saints*.

Religious texts were not the only works translated in early medieval Britain.[93] Secular texts were translated for enjoyment and entertainment, and early medieval scholars also sought out and promulgated knowledge by reading and translating works of learning. For instance, the *Historia Brittonum* was translated into Gaelic, in a text that has become known as the *Lebor Bretnach*. As Thomas Owen Clancy has convincingly argued, this translation first took place in northern Britain, in what is now Scotland, before subsequent recensions were copied in Ireland.[94] It is also important to remember that translation worked in both directions: for example, the text known as the *Chronicle of Æthelweard* is a tenth-century Latin translation of a now-lost Old English recension of the *Anglo-Saxon Chronicle*.

---

[91] Preface to the Old English translation of St Gregory's *Pastoral Care*; Sweet, *King Alfred's West Saxon Version of Gregory's Pastoral Care*.

[92] Old English: Stanton, *The Culture of Translation in Anglo-Saxon England*. Old Irish: Boyle, *History and Salvation in Medieval Ireland*.

[93] Olsen, Harbus and Hofstra, *Germanic Texts and Latin Models*.

[94] Clancy, 'Scotland, the "Nennian" Recension of the *Historia Brittonum*, and the *Lebor Bretnach*'.

At the same time as some scholars produced translations between Latin and early medieval Britain's various vernaculars, others introduced new languages into the island's intellectual milieu. We have already seen the importance of Old Irish to the formation of the early Anglo-Saxon church, particularly in Northumbria. Scattered throughout the early historical record are reminders of the continued frequency of this contact. For example, Bede's *Historia Ecclesiastica* includes the story of an Irish monk named Fursey, who became famous for his vision of the afterlife. Bede reports that he 'preached the word of God in Ireland for many years' until he 'left his native island' and 'came with a few companions through the land of the Britons and into the kingdom of the East Angles, where he preached the Word and there, as we have said, built a monastery'.[95] Bede makes no comment on Fursey's linguistic abilities, but from this narrative of his life, it is apparent that he was fluent in Old Irish and Old English as well as Latin. In fact, knowledge of a third vernacular is implied by the fact that after his time in East Anglia, Fursey spent the rest of his life in Frankish Gaul. Small moments such as the life of Fursey make clear the extent to which multilingualism was embedded into the fabric of intellectual and religious life in early medieval Britain. A few centuries later, for instance, as part of the entry for the year 891, the *Anglo-Saxon Chronicle* describes how some Irish *peregrini* came to find themselves in King Alfred's court:

> Three [Irishmen] came to King Alfred in a boat without any oars, from Ireland, where they had stolen away because they wanted for the love of God to be abroad – they did not care where. The boat in which they set out was made of two-and-a-half skins, and they took with them food for seven days; and after 7 days they came to land in Cornwall, and immediately went to King Alfred.[96]

We know nothing about these pilgrims beyond the information conveyed in this and subsequent chronicle entries, but this incident has often been noted as evidence in support of the prevalence of Irish scholars in Anglo-Saxon England. The episode underscores the same points as Fursey's narrative: though multilingualism itself is rarely commented upon in historical sources, inter-actions between individuals who spoke different vernaculars were common indeed. Moments such as these make clear that one or more of the parties involved must have been fluent in multiple languages in order for the interaction to take place as described.

Another language which held a prominent place in the intellectual climate of early medieval Britain was Greek. The study of Greek in early Anglo-Saxon

---

[95] Colgrave and Mynors, *Bede's Ecclesiastical History of the English People*, iii.19, 275.
[96] Swanton, *Anglo-Saxon Chronicle*, s.a. 891, 82.

England prospered under the influence of two scholars, Theodore and Hadrian, at Canterbury.[97] They have been credited with ushering in 'a golden age of learning in Anglo-Saxon England that was to be one of the high points of scholarship in the early Middle Ages'.[98] Theodore of Tarsus, who was later to become the Archbishop of Canterbury, was a native Greek speaker born in Tarsus, in what is now Turkey. When the Persians captured that city in the early seventh century, Theodore fled to Constantinople, where he gained a reputation as a learned scholar. He arrived in Rome by the second half of the seventh century, after the Synod of Whitby confirmed the Anglo-Saxon church's adherence to Roman methods of calculating Easter. Theodore was then chosen by Pope Vitalian upon the recommendation of Hadrian, a Greek-speaking native of North Africa, to fill the vacancy at Canterbury and consecrated as archbishop in 668. Immediately upon their arrival to Anglo-Saxon England, Theodore and Hadrian inaugurated a school at Canterbury that rapidly gained a reputation for world-class learning. The two men taught biblical exegesis and other scholarly subjects via Greek, Latin, and Syriac texts. In the first half of the eighth century, Bede noted that 'some of their students still survive who know Latin and Greek just as well as their native tongue'.[99] Theodore and Hadrian's school at Canterbury underscores not only the presence of speakers of other native languages in Anglo-Saxon England but also the value placed upon learning and teaching those languages to the intellectual community of early medieval Britain.

Theodore and Hadrian taught both 'sacred and secular literature', giving lessons 'not only in the books of holy Scripture but also in the art of metre, astronomy, and ecclesiastical computation'.[100] However, it is clear that to the Christian intellectual community of early medieval Britain, the most meaningful reason for teaching or learning Greek was so that one could get as close as possible to the original text of the Bible. The Bible was, of course, a highly fluid text, particularly in the early medieval period. But medieval scholars were aware of their distance from its 'original' language. The different texts that came together to compose 'the Bible' in its known form in the Middle Ages were first written in Hebrew, Aramaic, and Koine Greek. The Bible was then translated into Vulgar Latin by early Christian scholars during the late antique period, first in a stage known as the *Vetus Latina* which was then revised by fourth-century scholar Jerome into the *Vulgate*, and finally, into various vernaculars such as Old English in the early Middle Ages. A knowledge of Greek

---

[97] Lendinara, 'The World of Anglo-Saxon Learning'; Major, *Undoing Babel*, Ch 3.

[98] Major, *Undoing Babel*, 79.

[99] Colgrave and Mynors, *Bede's Ecclesiastical History of the English People*, iv.2, 335.

[100] Colgrave and Mynors, *Bede's Ecclesiastical History of the English People*, iv.2, 333–5.

meant that medieval scholars had closer access to the Bible in its original form, but by the extension of this principle, no language was more sacred than Hebrew. There were no Jewish communities in Anglo-Saxon England,[101] but there was some scholarly knowledge of Hebrew.[102] Thus, Bede's statement that there were five languages in early medieval Britain can actually be expanded. The 'saints and scholars' of the island's religious and intellectual communities embraced multilingualism as a crucial part of their spiritual and academic growth.

Because the vast majority of surviving evidence for multilingualism in early medieval Britain is written, the balance of this Element's discussions focuses on the most privileged medieval individuals: the tiny, elite, and nearly exclusively male and religious minority who were either capable of literacy and thus recording their own stories, or who were politically influential enough to have their stories recorded for them.[103] Some of this imbalance is addressed in Section 3's discussion of placenames as evidence for sustained oral contact between non-elite speakers of different languages, while Section 4 draws upon the broadest range of evidence possible to consider the role of multilingualism in the daily lives of those who do not feature in surviving written records. The genre of source material which contains the most anecdotal evidence for the lives of everyday people is hagiography (saints' lives), in the narratives recording their miracles. Yet even here, in order to think about the ways in which multilingualism is featured in the daily lives of non-elites, we must read between the lines of our sources. For example, when relating posthumous miracles that occurred on the site of the battle known as 'Maserfelth' where Northumbrian king-turned-saint Oswald was killed, Bede carefully includes the detail that 'another man, a Briton'[104] noticed the vibrancy of the patch of grass where Oswald died. The man took some of the soil with him, and its miraculous nature was duly proven later that night, when a house fire burned down everything except the post on which the bag containing the soil was hanging. The Briton in this story is given no direct lines of dialogue by Bede, but his ethnicity is noted. Implicit in this story, again, is the reality that someone – either the Briton himself, or an ecclesiastical witness to whom he reported the miracle – spoke at least two languages in order for the narrative

---

[101] Scheil, *The Footsteps of Israel*.

[102] Keefer and Burrows, 'Hebrew and the *Hebraicum* in late Anglo-Saxon England'.

[103] 'There are precious few documents or literary texts likely to be the work of laypeople', and of these, 'most examples related to the highest elite'; Naismith and Woodman, *Writing, Kingship and Power in Anglo-Saxon England*, 5; however, Insley, 'Archives and Lay Documentary Practice', has argued for a documentary culture that included the laity in Anglo-Saxon England.

[104] Colgrave and Mynors, *Bede's Ecclesiastical History of the English People*, iii.10, 245.

to have been preserved. While we do not have as comprehensive a record of the conversion of non-elites, surviving evidence suggests that multilingualism played an equally central role.

3 Kings and Captives

The conversion of the Anglo-Saxons to Christianity meant that they shared a knowledge of Latin, an awareness of its potential as a *lingua franca*, and a common sense of belonging to wider Latin Christendom with the other *gentes* living in early medieval Britain. However, this did not mean that multilingualism ceased to be a substantial factor in interactions between different peoples. Early medieval Britain was fairly unusual in how little direct influence its vernacular languages had upon one another.[105] Unlike analogous historical situations involving the settlement of one linguistic minority into the territory of a linguistic majority (such as the Vikings in Normandy), where settlers quickly adopted the language of their new homeland, the languages spoken in early medieval Britain remained distinct. All of the island's Celtic languages descend from a common ancestor (known as Proto-Celtic or common Celtic) and therefore share many words, morphological features, and syntactical patterns in common.[106] However, these ancestral commonalities are not the same as active linguistic influence during the early medieval period, which was limited to a small amount of linguistic borrowing between Welsh, Old English, and Latin. Leaving aside placenames for the moment, borrowings between Welsh and Old English are extremely rare and include a small handful of words such as that for 'badger' (Welsh *broch* to Old English *brocc*) and Welsh *edling* from Old English *ætheling* (a noble heir).[107] Latin influence on both languages was more obvious, as both Welsh and Old English borrowed terminology having to do with religion and education, such as Welsh *llyfr* (book, from Latin *liber*), *ysgol* (school, from Latin *schola*), and *eglwys* (church, from Latin *ecclesia*) and Old English words meaning wine (*win*, from Latin *vinum*), cross (*cros*, from Latin *crux*), mass (*mæsse*, from Latin *missa*), dish (*disc*, from Latin *discus*), and bishop (*biscop*, from Latin *episcopus*).[108] The vernaculars of early medieval Britain thus remained distinctive from one another in ways that made language a significant marker of ethnic identity. In practical terms, this meant that multilingualism was nearly always a factor in political negotiations between members of different *gentes*, as well as in negotiations between parties who would have considered themselves as

---

[105] Ward-Perkins, 'Why Did the Anglo-Saxons Not Become More British?'; but see Gretzinger et al., 'The Anglo-Saxon Migration and the Formation of the Early English Gene Pool'.
[106] Ball and Fife, *The Celtic Languages*.   [107] Parry-Williams, *The English Element in Welsh*.
[108] Miller, *External Influences on English*.

belonging to the same people, in situations where one party had spent a long period in exile.

This section will explore some of the practicalities, nuances, and long-term repercussions of multilingualism in the political sphere of early medieval Britain. In doing so, the discussion considers several key questions. How many languages would an 'average' king, diplomat, or soldier have known, and to what level of fluency? Who learned multiple vernacular languages in early medieval Britain, and how were they acquired? How was multilingualism valued by broader society: was knowing multiple languages treated as a valuable skill, or a straightforward part of everyday life? In what types of situations in the historical record is multilingualism commented upon as something noteworthy? What types of multilingualism existed across different social and political situations? Were there differences between the use of Latin as a *lingua franca* and direct translation between vernaculars? How did political prisoners, exiles, hostages, slaves, the parties in arranged marriages, and others who experienced varying degrees of non-consensual movement throughout the early medieval world function in multilingual environments?

From the earliest written sources of post-Roman Britain, it is clear that multilingualism played a prominent role in the political sphere. As we have seen, dual Latin and Gaelic inscribed monuments were used to commemorate influential figures, suggesting an audience to whom the use of both languages was significant. Yet the evidence provided by these stones is even more complex than it first appears. Some have Welsh names, making the corpus effectively trilingual, and these monuments are not evenly distributed throughout Britain but rather are found only in western regions where pockets of Irish Gaelic speakers settled.[109] Texts narrating the history of the early medieval period likewise preserve moments of linguistic contact between vernaculars that call attention to their role as markers of ethnic identity. For example, in his *De excidio*, describing the coming of the Anglo-Saxons to Britain, Gildas wrote: 'Then a pack of cubs burst forth from the lair of the barbarian lioness, coming in three *keels*, as they call warships in their language'.[110] Similarly, an episode in the *Historia Brittonum* describing how the Anglo-Saxons treacherously attacked the Britons after inviting them to a purported peace treaty relates that Anglo-Saxon leader 'Hengest told all his followers to hide their daggers under their feet in their shoes, saying "When I call out to you and say [in Old English] '*English, draw your knives*', take your daggers from your shoes and fall upon them, and stand firm against them"'.[111] Describing the construction of the

---

[109] Charles-Edwards, *Wales and the Britons*, 75–173; Edwards, 'Material Evidence and Identity'.

[110] Winterbottom, *Gildas*, 97 and 26.

[111] Morris, *Nennius*, 73 and 32; for discussion, Thomas, *History and Identity in Early Medieval Wales*, Ch. 2, 'Language'.

Antonine wall, Bede writes: 'It starts almost two miles west of the monastery at *Aebbercurnig* (Abercorn) in the place which the Picts call *Peanfahel*, while in English it is called *Penneltun* (Kinneil)'.[112] Speaking of bishop Colmán of Lindisfarne, Bede describes how he travelled from Iona 'to a small island some distance off the west coast of Ireland, called in Irish Inisboufinde (Inishbofin), the island of the white heifer'.[113] Asides such as these draw our attention to the different names that the different languages of early medieval Britain could have for the same location, and the ways in which these names were used reflect the linguistic landscape of a region. Multiple names for the same place, as in Bede's example, show multiple linguistic groups living side-by-side. When the most commonly recorded name of a given locale shifts from one language to another over time, we can hypothesise that the majority language spoken in that region has also shifted.[114] Placenames are often self-conscious indications of identity: a modern example is the Irish seaside town originally known as Dunleary (an anglicised spelling of a Gaelic placename), renamed 'Kingstown' after a visit by English king George IV in 1821, then renamed Dún Laoghaire (with Gaelicised spelling) in 1920 prior to the formation of the Irish Free State. Given the symbolic potential of placenames as reflections of political identity, instances where one language has naturally absorbed a placename from another have been understood to reflect sustained contact between speakers of those languages on a non-elite level. Moments such as the above testify to both the realities of multilingualism in early medieval Britain and its inhabitants' awareness that the languages they spoke were reflective of political identities.

We have already seen the ways in which Latin was incredibly useful as a *lingua franca* throughout western Christendom, and it was no less significant in facilitating communication within the economic and political spheres. In Britain, letters are preserved from as early as the Roman period in the form of the Vindolanda tablets, which are brief messages written in ink on thin pieces of wood.[115] In the Anglo-Saxon period, letters were inscribed into wax-covered wooden tablets, which could subsequently be erased by heating and smoothing the wax so that they could be reused, or written in ink on parchment.[116] Unsurprisingly, it is overwhelmingly the latter that survive, and most of these in turn are in Latin: extant letters in Old English are much rarer and date from later in the period. Original copies of letters were written on single sheets of

---

[112] Colgrave and Mynors, *Bede's Ecclesiastical History of the English People*, i.12, 43.

[113] Colgrave and Mynors, *Bede's Ecclesiastical History of the English People*, iv.4, 347.

[114] Parsons, 'Place-Names and Offa's Dyke'.

[115] Vindolanda Tablets Online, http://vindolanda.csad.ox.ac.uk/; Bowman, *Life and Letters on the Roman Frontier*.

[116] Zweck, *Epistolary Acts*, 26–32.

parchment which were folded shut. A few examples of single-sheet letters have been preserved, but because individual sheets of parchment were vulnerable to loss or damage, most extant letters from early medieval Britain survive because they were considered important enough to copy into cartularies or other codices.

Those letters which have been preserved illustrate the significance of Latin as a language of correspondence between key religious and political figures. Individuals for whom a significant body of written correspondence survives include St Boniface, an Anglo-Saxon missionary to Germanic kingdoms on the continent; Aldhelm, a scholar, poet, and eventual Abbot of Malmesbury, who studied with Theodore and Hadrian at Canterbury; and Alcuin of York, a Northumbrian scholar and poet who became a leading intellectual at the Carolingian court of Charlemagne. The latter's correspondence is particularly voluminous, as nearly 300 letters between Alcuin and other high-profile polit-ical, ecclesiastical, and intellectual figures survive.[117] A good illustration of the diplomatic potential of Latin as an intermediary language is provided by a famous set of correspondence between eighth-century rulers Offa, king of the Anglo-Saxon kingdom of Mercia, and Charlemagne, king of the Franks and Lombards and emperor from 800.[118] Within this correspondence, we first see a cautionary tale of diplomatic relations gone sour. Charlemagne had suggested a marriage between his son and Offa's daughter, but was offended at Offa's political overstretching when Offa returned with a counter-proposal that his son marry Charlemagne's daughter as well. Diplomatic relations were eventually repaired through the intervention of Alcuin and others, and a surviving letter from Charlemagne to Offa, written in 796, encompasses a range of economic concerns: diplomatic gifts, Anglo-Saxon pilgrims and exiles on the continent, and trade between the Anglo-Saxons and the Franks, noting specifically cloth sent from Anglo-Saxon England to the continent and black stones which were exported in the opposite direction.

Within Anglo-Saxon England, multilingualism involving Latin also played a significant role in the writing of charters, which were brief documents preserving legal transactions such as the transfer of land from one party to another. As is the case with the corpus of surviving letters, the bulk of surviving charters from Anglo-Saxon England were written largely in Latin. However, the charters themselves were frequently multilingual documents in which the generic legal formulae were written in Latin, but specific details pertaining to the individual issue at hand were in the vernacular. For instance, it is extremely common to find charters with legal formulae in Latin but boundary descriptions of a given piece of land in Old English. The names of manumitted individuals

---

[117] Bullough, *Alcuin*; Dales, *Alcuin*.   [118] Story, 'Charlemagne and the Anglo-Saxons'.

and the contents of households to be dispersed in wills are also frequently found in the vernacular, as are the names of witnesses to all these types of legal agreements.[119] Yet this pattern is not consistent: as Annina Seiler has noted, 'spelling can be used to either highlight or downplay the vernacular character of the name'.[120] Surviving legal and political documents from early medieval Britain make clear that multilingualism, particularly that combining Latin and the vernacular, was a widely used tool that facilitated effective communication not only between individuals from different *gentes* and regions, but also across time, as documents such as charters were written and preserved with a deliberate eye towards posterity.

However, those who were able to write in Latin were an elite minority in early medieval Britain. Even those individuals with the highest degree of Latin fluency would not have absorbed it as a native tongue from birth, but rather would have been taught the language in a classroom context upon entering a monastic community at age seven.[121] There is no evidence that Latin continued as a spoken everyday language in Britain after the arrival of the Anglo-Saxons: it was not a living language outside of a monastic context, nor was it anyone's mother tongue. During most encounters between speakers of two different vernacular languages, it would have been easier to translate directly than to use Latin as an intermediary. The necessity of interpreters was also recognised during political negotiations. For example, the *Historia Brittonum* makes a point of noting the presence of an interpreter during its narrative of the pseudohistorical early encounters between the Anglo-Saxons and the Britons immediately after the former's arrival in Britain. The text describes how Anglo-Saxon leader Hengest tempted British leader Vortigern with his beautiful daughter, relating that, 'Hengest held a banquet for Vortigern, and his men and his interpreter, whose name was Ceretic, and he told the girl to serve their wine and spirits'.[122] Although this story is legendary, it underscores the widespread awareness within early medieval Britain that two peoples speaking different vernaculars and engaged in political negotiations would have required the aid of an interpreter, a profession for which we have good historical evidence.[123] A range of similar episodes took place in reality, from the political

---

[119] Howe, *Writing the Map of Anglo-Saxon England*; Gallagher, Roberts, and Tinti, *The Languages of Early Medieval Charters*.

[120] Seiler, 'Germanic Names, Vernacular Sounds, and Latin Spellings in Early Anglo-Saxon and Alemannic Charters', 147.

[121] While some medieval clergy took a second Christian name, many kept their birth names, which provide valuable evidence of their cultural background: Wilson, *The Means of Naming*, 94.

[122] Morris, *Nennius*, 28.

[123] Suppe, 'Interpreter Families and Anglo-Welsh Relations in the Shropshire–Powys Marches in the Twelfth Century'; Suppe, 'Who Was Rhys Sais?'; Crick, '"The English" and "The Irish" from Cnut to John'; Aird, 'Interpreting the King's Will'.

alliance between the pagan Anglo-Saxon king Penda of Mercia and the Christian British king Cadwallon of Gwynedd[124] to the disastrously divisive conference between British bishops and Augustine and Æthelberht.[125] While Bede's *Historia Ecclesiastica*, where these episodes are recorded, makes no direct comment on the linguistic features of such scenes, the reality of historical moments such as these is that people had to understand one another in order to form political alliances or conduct theological debates, and perceived linguistic boundaries were often porous.

How did interpreters learn more than one language? Section 4 considers travel and trade, but three scenarios – exile, hostageship, and politically advantageous exogamous marriages – represent some of the most widespread opportunities within the political sphere. We have already seen that Northumbrian king Oswald served as an interpreter for Irish bishop Aidan due to his Gaelic fluency gained in exile.[126] It was an experience he shared with many other politically vulnerable young men, including his brothers, as 'during the whole of Edwin's reign the sons of King Æthelfrith his predecessor, together with many young nobles, were living in exile among the Irish or the Picts where they were instructed in the faith as the Irish taught it'.[127] Nor were Irish and Pictish the only languages learnt. The eighth-century *Life of Saint Guthlac* narrates the biography of the titular saint, who was born into a noble Mercian family in 674 and spent his early life as a successful warrior until a change of heart at age twenty-four prompted him to abandon his heroic lifestyle and enter the monastery at Repton. In 699, he left the monastery to live as a hermit in the Fens, where he remained until his death in 715. His *Life* relates that at one point during his hermitage, Guthlac was attacked by demons appearing in the guise of Britons: 'he recognized the words that the crowd were saying, and realized that British hosts were approaching his dwelling: for in years gone by he had been an exile among them, so that he was able to understand their sibilant speech'.[128] The period of time spent in exile was usually a significant one, and the fact that exile was the default option for those too young to rule in their own right made the acquisition of a second vernacular language a likely outcome. Exiles were of significant enough birth to be a political threat, meaning that exile facilitated multilingualism within the political landscape of early medieval Britain.

Another group that acquired second languages in the political sphere were those exchanged (or seized) as hostages.[129] Hostages could be voluntarily given as a promise of good conduct, such as when one king submitted to a more

---

[124] *HE* ii.20.   [125] *HE* ii.2.

[126] Colgrave and Mynors, *Bede's Ecclesiastical History of the English People*, iii.3, 221.

[127] Colgrave and Mynors, *Bede's Ecclesiastical History of the English People*, iii.1, 213.

[128] Colgrave, *Felix's Life of Saint Guthlac*, ch. xxxiv, 111.

[129] Kosto, *Hostages in the Middle Ages*.

powerful one. They could also be taken as captives after a defeat, or exchanged to solidify a truce. The opportunities for language acquisition as a hostage were similar to those of an exile in that hostages often spent long periods of time living alongside those who held them. In 757, the *Anglo-Saxon Chronicle*[130] records a deadly feud between the retainers of two Anglo-Saxon leaders, Cynewulf and Cyneheard. During the first round of a climactic battle between the two groups, 'they were fighting continuously until they were all killed, except for one British hostage, and he was very wounded'.[131] This British hostage fought and most likely died alongside his Anglo-Saxon household, and though the *Anglo-Saxon Chronicle* makes no mention of it, he would have needed to be able to speak Old English in order to do so. Similar episodes of implied multilingualism are evident throughout the historical record. For example, queen Æthelflæd – described by the *Anglo-Saxon Chronicle* as the 'Lady of the Mercians', who ruled that kingdom from the death of her husband Æthelred in 911 until her own death in 918 – 'sent an army into Wales and broke down Brecon Mere, and there took the wife of the king as one of thirty-four'.[132] This brief annal omits any description of what took place after the raid, but in this and similar instances, someone must have been able to communicate across the Anglo/Welsh linguistic boundary, perhaps via the intermediary of Latin, in order to negotiate the hostages' release.[133] After the arrival of the Vikings to Britain and Ireland, high-profile hostages were frequently captured and ransomed for profit. Ransom involved multilingual negotiations. For instance, St Findán (St Fintan) was born in Ireland at the beginning of the ninth century. After being sold abroad by Vikings, he escaped and travelled widely across continental Europe before in 851 joining the monastery at Rheinau, Switzerland, where he lived until his death in 878. His biography, the *Vita Sancti Findani*, was written by a contemporary at Rheinau shortly after his death. Findán's *Vita* relates that his first encounter with the Vikings came after his sister was captured and held for ransom. Then, their father 'instructed his son Findan to take a sum of money, ransom his sister, and bring her back to him', which Findán did, 'taking with him some followers and an interpreter'.[134] The capture, maintenance, and ransom of hostages between different *gentes* required the use of interpreters to facilitate communication, and a long period of time

---

[130] A shorthand for seven surviving manuscripts of the same text, which originated in a Common Stock written during the late-ninth-century court of King Alfred but diverged in tone, style, and content when they were disseminated and continued at separate locations across Anglo-Saxon England: see Stafford, *After Alfred.*

[131] Swanton, *Anglo-Saxon Chronicle, MS E*, s.a. 755 [757], 49.

[132] Swanton, *Anglo-Saxon Chronicle, MS C*, s.a. 916, 100.

[133] Benham, *Peacemaking in the Middle Ages*; Lane and Redknap, *Llangorse Crannog.*

[134] Christiansen, 'The People of the North', 156.

spent as a hostage may very well have been the way in which some of those interpreters originally acquired a second language.

Another scenario in which speakers of two vernacular languages came into close and extended contact with one another was when exogamous marriages (that is, marriages in which one party came from outside a given cultural, religious, or kin group) occurred. Sometimes, such marriages were arranged for politically advantageous purposes, but in other instances, they appear to have formed naturally. 'Ferr soben socheníul' (Better a good wife than an exalted family), proclaims a proverb from the Old Irish text known as 'The Sayings of Flann Fína son of Oswiu'.[135] Flann Fína was another name for Aldfrith, king of Northumbria from 685 until his death in 704 or 705. Personal names are important reflections of linguistic interactions in the political sphere, and the bilingual names of Aldfrith/Flann Fína suggest that he viewed his Anglo-Saxon and Irish heritage as equally valid. Aldfrith was the son of Oswiu of Bernicia – himself one of the sons of Æthelfrith of Northumbria, who as noted above, spent significant time in exile during his youth – and an Irish princess named Fín or Fína from the northern Uí Néill dynasty. Oswiu had three known wives: the Irish Fín/Fína; a British princess, Rhiennmelt of Rheged; and his third wife, the Anglo-Saxon queen Eanflæd.[136] Aldfrith was raised in an Irish-speaking environment in the kingdom of the Dál Riata, which stretched across the Irish Sea, encompassing parts of the regions that now form Northern Ireland and Scotland, and a rich historical tradition exists about him in early Irish sources, including the attribution of the aforementioned proverbs to his authorship.[137] The arrangement of politically advantageous exogamous marriages was also quite common in Anglo-Saxon England. In the early period, 'the adoption of British name-elements by the West Saxon royal house may indicate that intermarriage and alliances with leading British families helped West Saxon assimilation of British territory'.[138] Naming patterns could also reflect political relationships, as when increased contact between Welsh kings and the West Saxon court during the ninth and tenth centuries led to an increase in Anglo-Saxon names bestowed upon Welsh children, Hywel Dda's son Edwin being the most famous example. Marriage alliances between the royal families of Anglo-Saxon kingdoms, or between Anglo-Saxon and British, Irish, or Pictish dynasties, were extremely common.[139] Another of Oswald's and

---

[135] Ireland, *Old Irish Wisdom Attributed to Aldfrith of Northumbria*, 84–5, §6.59.

[136] Grimmer, 'The Exogamous Marriages of Oswiu of Northumbria'.

[137] Ireland, 'Aldfrith of Northumbria and the Irish Genealogies'.

[138] Yorke, *Kings and Kingdoms of Early Anglo-Saxon England*, 155.

[139] Cessford, 'Exogamous Marriages Between Anglo-Saxons and Britons in Seventh Century Northern Britain'; Lancaster, 'Kinship in Anglo-Saxon Society'.

Oswiu's brothers, Eanfrith of Bernicia, married a Pictish princess during his exile. She gave birth to their son, Talorgan, who later became king of the Picts from 653 to 657.

Relationships such as Oswiu's and Eanfrith's may have formed naturally during the course of their exiles. At the highest political level, many prominent Anglo-Saxon kings married the daughters of royal families on the continent, with an eye to forming advantageous political connections. Some of the most famous pairings include the Frankish Bertha and the Anglo-Saxon Æthelberht of Kent, whom we have already met (sixth century); the Carolingian Judith of Flanders and the Anglo-Saxon Æthelwulf of Wessex (ninth century); and the Norman Emma of Normandy with first the Anglo-Saxon king Æthelred 'the unready' and then the Danish king Cnut (early eleventh century); as well as Mercian king Offa's failed attempt to marry his son Ecgfrith to Charlemagne's daughter Bertha (eighth century), discussed above. As we have seen from Bede's description of Bertha and Æthelbert's marriage, these high-status individuals did not come to Britain by themselves but brought households and retinues with them, all of whom would have created pockets of multilingual communities in the locations of their arrival. Moreover, as Aldfrith's case illustrates, exogamous marriages resulted in linguistic exchange not only between spouses, but also between parents and children.

Slaves played a significant but involuntary role shaping early medieval Britain's multilingual landscape.[140] The history of slavery in Britain dates at least back to the time of the Roman empire,[141] and most likely before, though written records from that period are not extant. After the arrival of the Anglo-Saxons to Britain, and again after the arrival of the Vikings, pre-existing patterns of raiding and slave trading gained a new layer of linguistic complexity which was acknowledged in the written records of the time. For example, the Old English word *wealh* originally meant 'slave' or 'foreigner', and came to designate 'the Welsh' specifically over the course of the Anglo-Saxon period.[142] An awareness of ethnic differences between Britons and Anglo-Saxons can be seen in texts such as a law code issued by Ine, king of Wessex from the late seventh to early eighth centuries, which draws a sharp distinction in the value of *wergild* (monetary compensation for death or injury) in Britons and Anglo-Saxons of equivalent social rank.[143]

---

[140] Pelteret, *Slavery in Early Mediaeval England*; Wyatt, *Slaves and Warriors in Medieval Britain and Ireland*.

[141] Joshel, *Slavery in the Roman World*; Rio, *Slavery after Rome*.

[142] Faull, 'The Semantic Development of Old English *Wealh*'; Brady, 'The "Dark Welsh" as Slaves and Slave Traders'.

[143] Grimmer, 'Britons in Early Wessex' and Woolf, 'Apartheid Economics in Anglo-Saxon England'.

The arrival of the Vikings to the insular region expanded the scope of the slave trade in Britain and Ireland from internal raiding between kingdoms to profit-driven trading overseas.[144] Texts such as the *Vita Sancti Findani* noted above underscore the linguistic differences and harsh realities of Viking capture and slavery, as well as the involuntary mobility that could come about as a result of such encounters. Alongside the biography of St Findán, a handful of slightly later texts, most explicitly the early eleventh-century satirical Norman poem *Moriuht* and the thirteenth-century Icelandic *Laxdæla saga*,[145] provide fictional yet plausibly realistic accounts of what the experiences of those captured by Vikings may have been like. Though its primary setting is Iceland rather than Britain, *Laxdæla saga* is of particular note because one of its foundational characters, Melkorka, is the daughter of an Irish king who was captured and sold on the slave market. A key plot point in the saga is that she chooses not to speak to her Icelandic buyer and rapist, but secretly teaches their son Old Irish so that he may eventually reclaim ties with his maternal family. The high percentage of maternally derived Celtic ancestry in Iceland's genealogical and genetic records has been much-discussed,[146] and while *Laxdæla saga* itself is a work of what we might call historical fiction, it nonetheless depicts a believable account of the lived experience of slavery among another people. While slaves were the lowest social class and their stories are therefore largely absent from written historical records, texts like *Laxdæla saga* show medieval awareness that slaves were taken far from their homelands, spoke different languages than their captors, and passed those languages on to their children.

Historical records can reveal the lived realities of communities where multi-lingualism likely existed on a daily basis. In early medieval Britain, the two most long-standing such regions were the Anglo-Welsh borderlands and the Danelaw. An Old English legal text known as the *Dunsæte Agreement* or *Ordinance concerning the Dunsæte* gives us rare first-hand insight into some of the practicalities of living in a multilingual community along the Anglo-Welsh borderlands.[147] The *Dunsæate Agreement* appears to be an unofficial memorandum of understanding drawn up within this community rather than an official royal law code.[148] The brief document outlines a series of mutually

---

[144] Bromberg, 'Wales and the Mediaeval Slave Trade'; Charles, *Old Norse Relations with Wales*; Holm, 'The Slave Trade of Dublin, Ninth to Twelfth Centuries'; Duffy, 'Ostmen, Irish and Welsh in the Eleventh Century'; Etchingham, 'North Wales, Ireland and the Isles: The Insular Viking Zone'.

[145] McDonough, *Warner of Rouen, Moriuht*; Kunz, *Saga of the People of Laxardal*.

[146] Helgason et al., 'mtDNA and the Origin of the Icelanders'; Helgason et al., 'Estimating Scandinavian and Gaelic Ancestry in the Male Settlers of Iceland'; Helgason et al., 'mtDNA and the Islands of the North Atlantic'.

[147] Brady, *Writing the Welsh borderlands*, 1–6 and 16–19.

[148] Text from Liebermann, *Die Gesetze der Angelsachsen*, I, 358–63, by clause and line number.

agreed-upon procedures for addressing cattle theft and its aftermath in a community comprised of a mixed Welsh and Anglo-Saxon population, through which a river ran: the text's prologue states, 'This is the agreement which the advisers of the English (*Angelcynnes witan*) and the counsellors of the Welsh (*Wealhþeode rædboran*) put in place among the Dunsæte'.[149] The approximate location of the territory of the *Dunsæte* can be narrowed down to the River Wye between Monmouth and Hereford from the *Agreement*'s final clause.[150] George Molyneaux has dated this text to the late tenth or eleventh centuries,[151] and it has been well-studied as a reflection of both shared legal obligations and a series of practical steps to keep the peace within a borderland community.[152]

We know nothing about this community apart from the information in the *Dunsæte Agreement* itself, but the details it reveals both suggest some of the practicalities underlying how a multilingual community would have functioned and raise intriguing questions. We know that the community's Welsh and Anglo-Saxon inhabitants lived on opposite banks of the river, but also that men living in different districts appear to have frequently colluded with one another in cattle theft.[153] We don't know what language the 'Angelcynnes witan and Wealhþeode rædboran' used to communicate – Old English, Welsh, Latin or some other *lingua franca* – or indeed, in what language this document was first drafted. The *Dunsæte Agreement* is written in Old English and preserved in one copy in Cambridge, Corpus Christi College MS 383, an early twelfth-century compilation of Anglo-Saxon legal material, and it later became one of the many Old English legal documents translated into Latin as part of the *Quadripartitus*.[154] Could there have been an original Latin copy of the *Dunsæte Agreement*, or perhaps a Welsh version parallel to the Old English? The *Agreement* describes how 'twelve lawmen (*lahmen*) shall proclaim what is just for Welsh and English: six Englishmen and six Welshmen'.[155] Who were these *lahmen*? The word is a Scandinavian borrowing known only from this text, although its Latinate equivalent, *lagemanni*, appears in a few legal documents written after 1066.[156] Were they the same people as the 'Angelcynnes witan and Wealhþeode rædboran' who drafted the *Dunsæte Agreement*? Could anyone living within the Dunsæte territory be a *lahmann*, or did these men hold

---

[149] *Dunsæte Prologue.*

[150] *Dunsæte* 9,1. See Gelling, *The West Midlands in the Early Middle Ages*, 112–19.

[151] Molyneaux, '*The Ordinance Concerning the Dunsæte*'.

[152] Fordham, 'Peacekeeping and Order on the Anglo-Welsh Frontier'; Brady, *Writing the Welsh borderlands.*

[153] *Dunsæte* 6,1 and 6,3.   [154] Wormald, *The Making of English Law*, 228–44.

[155] *Dunsæte* 3,3.   [156] Molyneaux, '*The Ordinance Concerning the Dunsæte*', 262–5.

permanent positions as legal advisers to their community? If so, were they more likely than their neighbours to be able to speak more than one language?[157]

Despite the many questions this document raises, the *Dunsæte Agreement* reveals a community that worked together to solve its problems, had a system of legal rights and responsibilities for all its members, and possessed a functional level of both linguistic and legal comprehension between its Anglo-Saxon and Welsh inhabitants. Even though the surviving text is written in Old English, the *Dunsæte Agreement* reflects Anglo-Welsh equality at every turn. Its penultimate clause takes care to emphasise that 'likewise must an Englishman undertake what is right for a Welshman';[158] the legal principles it contains represent a fusion of Welsh and Anglo-Saxon customs; and the *Agreement* is designed to quickly settle potential feuds and promote peace in the community. It is clear that some level of multilingualism must have been present within the territory of the Dunsæte in order for the community to function in the ways outlined in the *Agreement*.

Indeed, an easy-to-overlook detail in the final clause of this text further emphasises the importance of multilingualism within this region. The text states that:

> at one point the *Wentsæte* belonged to the *Dunsæate*, but the territory of the *Wentsæte* belongs more rightly to the West Saxons. The *Wentsæte* ought to give tribute and hostages to the West Saxons. Even so, the *Dunsæte* think it necessary – if the king will grant it to the *Dunsæte* – that at least hostages for peace from the *Wentsæte* may be permitted to the *Dunsæte*.[159]

The *Wentsæte* are the people of Gwent, a Welsh kingdom,[160] and the *Agreement*'s final clause reveals that they have recently shifted from being a client territory of a mixed Anglo-Welsh region (the *Dunsæte*) to an Anglo-Saxon one (the West Saxons). The example of the *Wentsæte* serves as an illustration of the much more widely known practice that Anglo-Saxon kingdoms frequently took tributes and hostages from Welsh territories. As Rebecca Thomas has argued, it is not insignificant that the Anglo-Saxon settlements with alternative Welsh placenames in early medieval texts were often administrative centres, such as Cirencester (Caer Geri), where tax collectors were based according to *Armes Prydein Vawr*.[161] It is possible that these Welsh placenames

---

[157] It is noteworthy that the Welsh laws state that an exile (*anghyfiaith*), someone 'not of the same language' – that is, who cannot speak Welsh – can have someone speak for them in court: Emanuel, *The Latin Texts of the Welsh Laws*, 354 and Thomas, 'Ysytr *anghyfiaith* mewn testunau Cymraeg Canol', 75–96.

[158] *Dunsæte* 8,4.   [159] *Dunsæte* 9,1. See further Brady, 'The Fluidity of Borderlands'.

[160] Gelling, *The West Midlands in the Early Middle Ages*, 118.

[161] Thomas, *History and Identity in Early Medieval Wales*, Ch. 2, 'Language'.

developed or were more widely used because of the political importance of these locations, reminding us of both the close relationship between linguistic and political identities in early medieval Britain but also that, like the territory of the Dunsæte, one place could be inhabited by multiple linguistic groups.

Another region where multiple languages coexisted over a sustained period of time was the area known as the Danelaw.[162] Viking-Age Britain had three distinct periods. Initially, from the late eighth to mid-ninth centuries, raids on wealthy coastal communities (largely monastic) were carried out during the summer, and the Vikings returned to Scandinavia by the autumn, as winter conditions were too dangerous for sailing. The second phase (mid-ninth century), known as 'overwintering', involved the construction of temporary encampments occupied by increasingly large armies over the winter months. These encampments not only enabled Viking armies to raid throughout the year, but also served as bases from which campaigns could be directed inland. Finally, from the later ninth century onwards, the third and final phase was one of settlement. The first and most significant Viking settlement in Britain was at York after their capture of that city, and the expanded area of settlement under Viking control, which grew to encompass large swaths of the kingdoms of Northumbria, East Anglia, and Mercia, eventually became known as the Danelaw. As was also the case with other kingdoms in early medieval Britain, the geographical extent of the Danelaw was never formally mapped. As Lesley Abrams notes, the term 'has been employed in a variety of ways, meaning a range of different things'.[163] For our purposes, 'the Danelaw' refers to the region of Britain where Scandinavians were recognised to have settled during the early medieval period and where Old English and Old Norse were spoken alongside one another.

The settlement of the Norse-speaking Vikings in Britain reshaped the island's multilingual landscape in several ways.[164] Due to the long inhabitation of the Danelaw, many Old Norse words were borrowed into the Old English language, specifically what has been characterised as 'homely' vocabulary: terminology for types of food, family relationships, common household tools and objects, adjectives, and clothing. Contact with Old Norse also simplified Old English grammatical inflexions so that the two languages could become more mutually intelligible. Moreover, the presence of the Vikings in Britain added another layer of multilingualism to political negotiations. The first surviving written record of the rights and responsibilities that Vikings and Anglo-Saxons had towards one another is the late ninth-century document known as the *Treaty of*

---

[162] Hadley, *The Northern Danelaw.*   [163] Abrams, 'Edward the Elder's Danelaw', 128.
[164] Lavelle and Roffey, *Danes in Wessex.*

Alfred and Guthrum, by which point it is clear that the Vikings were forming permanent communities in Britain. Similarly to the *Dunsæte Agreement*, while the *Treaty of Alfred and Guthrum* survives only in an Old English version that was later copied out in Latin as part of the *Quadripartitus*, it is clear that both Vikings and Anglo-Saxons were active parties in the *Treaty*'s negotiation and must have been able to understand the final document.

A Viking presence in the Danelaw persisted for two-hundred years after this treaty was signed. Old Norse took on an even more significant political role after 1003, when Danish king Sweyn Forkbeard first invaded Anglo-Saxon England in a series of campaigns. His efforts culminated in a wholesale victory in 1013, after which he was crowned as king. Sweyn died in 1014, but his son Cnut seized the throne in 1016, and his dynasty would rule until 1042. Cnut's court was a publicly and cannily multilingual one, continuing the strategies of earlier Viking rulers in the Danelaw who had, for example, issued coins inscribed with the Latin language and alphabet and containing Christian imagery.[165] The career of one of Cnut's chief advisors, Wulfstan, Archbishop of York, fittingly illustrates the multilingualism of later Anglo-Saxon England. Wulfstan was a prolific homilist who wrote in both Latin and Old English, a duality reflected in his most famous work, the *Sermo Lupi ad Anglos* ('The Sermon of the Wolf to the English') – an Old English homily with a Latin title.[166] This text, written in the early eleventh century, blames the sins of the Anglo-Saxons for the looming threat of the Vikings in Britain. Ironically, after Cnut's victory in 1016, Wulfstan managed to find himself a seat on the other side of the table, drafting the new king's law codes. Once Cnut was crowned, he quickly issued a series of documents in Old English. As Elaine Treharne has demonstrated, they proclaimed his 'legitimization and transformation' from 'Viking usurper to authorized Christian emperor'.[167] Wulfstan's later writings are notable not only as a reflection of his political acumen, but also for the significant Old Norse vocabulary they contain, underscoring the pervasive linguistic influence of the Danish community in Britain during Cnut's reign.[168] At the same time, a more elite strand of Old Norse, particularly in the form of notoriously dense and allusive skaldic poetry performed for public entertainment, was given a prominent place at Cnut's court.[169] While Old English and Old Norse were mutually intelligible on the level of basic conversation, that comprehensibility

---

[165] Williams, 'Kingship, Christianity, and Coinage'.

[166] Townend, *Wulfstan, Archbishop of York*.   [167] Treharne, *Living Through Conquest*, 34.

[168] Townend, *Language and History in Viking Age England*; Pons-Sanz, *Norse-Derived Vocabulary in Late Old English Texts*.

[169] Frank, 'King Cnut in the Verse of his Skalds'; Townend, 'Contextualizing the *Knútsdrápur*' and 'Cnut's poets'.

did not extend to the tangled syntax and complex layers of mythological references that skaldic poetry possessed. Thus, multilingualism at Cnut's court formed registers of privilege within the political sphere, in which full understanding of Old Norse signalled belonging to the ruling class.

4 Travellers and Traders

Most of the case studies examined up until this point have been drawn from those privileged members of society whose activities comprise the bulk of our surviving written records. How did multilingualism impact the lives of non-elites in early medieval Britain? Popular perception has held that it did not. Exposure to multiple languages has been associated with the ability to travel, which in turn has been understood as limited to either the mass migration of a people or to an upper class with the knowledge and means to organise their own journeys. It is assumed that during the medieval period, 'most people did not travel widely . . . there were multitudes whose only experience of the world ended a day's walk from the villages where they were born'.[170] The average medieval individual has been thought to have no exposure to any language other than their native tongue. How true are such assumptions, and how much evidence exists for the impact of multilingualism on the lives of non-elites? To answer these questions, this section explores the mobility of figures such as travellers and traders in order to think about the mechanisms by which multilingualism in early Britain extended beyond the upper classes.

When considering multilingualism in the context of travellers and traders, our story again begins in Roman Britain. The Roman Empire was a multilingual and multicultural institution that encompassed individuals from a wide range of backgrounds.[171] The geographic scope and scale of the Empire meant that its trade routes spanned the known world,[172] and thus, the economy of the Roman Empire did not merely facilitate moments of multilingual interaction, it was dependent upon them. Roman Britain participated in and benefitted from the Empire's vast trade network, but many of these connections collapsed alongside the western Empire in the fifth century.[173] Flourishing trade routes persisted throughout the Anglo-Saxon period: recall the letter from Charlemagne to Offa discussed in Section 3. It may seem an obvious point, but it is worth emphasising that traders from different regions of the early medieval world would not have spoken the same languages, yet they were clearly able to communicate with one another, as well as with people living in the communities they passed

---

[170] Smith, *The Cartographic Imagination*, 17.
[171] Price, Finkelberg, and Shahar, *Rome: An Empire of Many Nations*.
[172] Wilson and Bowman, *Trade, Commerce, and the State in the Roman World*.
[173] Fleming, *The Material Fall of Roman Britain*.

through. Coinage is a good source of physical evidence for the extent to which trade in the early medieval period took place across perceived linguistic and geographical boundaries.[174] In a slightly later period, around the eleventh century, there is good evidence for how such communication would have taken place. While the term has come to signify any system of communication between two individuals who do not speak a common language, the original *lingua franca* 'emerged in the Levant as an outcome of the trading contacts in the eastern Mediterranean Sea in the medieval period'.[175] It was a pidgin language spoken among traders from the ninth century onwards which became 'the language of commerce of all Mediterranean merchants and seamen in the later Middle Ages' – a situation which must have had many parallels elsewhere, but the first for which good evidence exists.[176] While no written evidence of traders' pidgins survives from early medieval Britain, merchants from a range of linguistic backgrounds must have been able to communicate with one another in order for trade to have taken place.

One group of merchants or traders from another linguistic background whom we know to have had a significant presence in Britain from fairly early in the Anglo-Saxon period are the Frisians. The Frisians came from a geographic region that now encompasses the coastal areas of the Netherlands and north-western Germany, and there is good historical evidence for their movements in the early medieval period and contacts with other peoples.[177] Indeed, 'historical Frisians are undoubtedly considered maritime people, both by their contemporaries and by present-day scholars, and are distinctively portrayed as connected to the North Sea once known as *Mare Frisicum*',[178] and 'it seems likely that there was already regular trade from the Low Countries in Anglo-Saxon times'.[179] Material evidence for the presence of Frisian traders has recently been augmented by Arjen P. Versloot's argument for the existence of a shared 'North Sea Germanic idiom',[180] which would have facilitated communication between speakers of Germanic languages living in northern coastal regions.

In Anglo-Saxon England, there is also good written historical evidence for both the presence of Frisians in the early medieval period and the fact that they were recognised as a distinctive group linked to trading and maritime activity.[181] Bede records the story of an Anglo-Saxon named Imma, of noble background, who in 679 was captured in war and sold 'to a Frisian in

---

[174] Naismith, 'Bige Habban'.   [175] Han, 'Trade migration and language', 266.
[176] Han, 'Trade migration and language', 266.
[177] Hines and IJssennagger-van der Pluijm, *Frisians of the Early Middle Ages*.
[178] IJssennagger-van der Pluijm, 'Structured by the Sea', 249.
[179] Owen-Crocker, 'Brides, Donors, Traders', 69.
[180] Versloot, 'Traces of a North Sea Germanic Idiom'.
[181] Bremmer, 'Frisians in Anglo-Saxon England'.

London'.[182] Due to the strong associations elsewhere in the historical record between Frisians and trading, most scholars have understood the Frisian in question to be a slave trader. Other mentions of Frisians link them to seafaring, as in 897, when the *Anglo-Saxon Chronicle* recorded that King Alfred ordered a specific type of ship to be built in order to fight the Vikings. These ships 'were neither of Frisian design nor of Danish, but as it seemed to himself they might be more useful'.[183] After the ships were built, in a naval battle between Anglo-Saxon and Viking forces, many men were killed. The *Anglo-Saxon Chronicle* names among the deceased 'Wulfheard the Frisian, and Æbbe the Frisian, and Æthelhere the Frisian ... and of all men, Frisian and English, 62'.[184] It is clear from episodes such as these that Frisians were recognised as a distinct group in early medieval Britain and that they were able to communicate with their Anglo-Saxon contemporaries well enough to trade with them and fight alongside them. Old Frisian was the most closely related Germanic language to Old English,[185] and scholars have hypothesised that the two languages were mutually intelligible in the early medieval period.[186]

There also appears to have been a substantial Frisian community established in York by the eighth century. The *Life* of eighth-century missionary Liudger, who was remembered for his efforts in converting the pagan Frisians and Saxons on the continent, includes a detailed episode of unrest between Frisians and Anglo-Saxons, which forced Liudger to flee from York, where he had gone to study with Alcuin, for his own safety. Liudger's ninth-century biographer Altfrid describes how: 'when the citizens went out to fight against their enemies, it happened that in the strife the son of a certain noble of that province was killed by a Frisian merchant, and therefore the Frisians hastened to leave the land of the English, fearing the wrath of the kindred of the slain young man'.[187] This episode is noteworthy not only for its confirmation of a substantial Frisian population in York, but also because it suggests that Frisians were perceived as a distinctive group, identifiable in some way to their Anglo-Saxon neighbours. While Old English and Old Frisian were closely related languages that were likely near-intelligible in the early medieval period, it is nonetheless still the likeliest explanation that spoken Frisian was distinctive enough to identify the community on a linguistic basis. Liudger is neither a merchant nor living in a Frisian neighbourhood, but is nonetheless sent from

---

[182] Colgrave and Mynors, *Bede's Ecclesiastical History of the English People*, iv.22, 405.

[183] Swanton, *Anglo-Saxon Chronicle, MS A*, s.a. 897, 90.

[184] Swanton, *Anglo-Saxon Chronicle, MS A*, s.a. 897, 91.

[185] Robinson, *Old English and Its Closest Relatives*.

[186] Mostert, 'Linguistics of Contact in the Northern Seas'.

[187] Altfrid, *Vita Sancti Liudgeri*, ch. 11; trans. Whitelock, *English Historical Documents*, 839–40.

York due to Alcuin's fear that he will be harmed on account of his Frisian identity. Altfrid's *Life* notes that: 'compelled by necessity, Alcuin sent Liudger with the aforesaid merchants, and with him his deacon, Pyttel by name, for he was afraid that Liudger in his love of learning would go to another city of that region and suffer some attack in vengeance for the aforesaid young man'.[188] In sum, then, Liudger's biography provides evidence of a settled and substantial Frisian population, most of whom were likely to have been merchants or traders, who were recognised as identifiably distinct from their Anglo-Saxon contemporaries. While references to Frisians in the Anglo-Saxon period are not as widespread as are those to speakers of the British, Gaelic, or Norse languages, it is nonetheless clear that Frisians represented another distinctive linguistic community which had a significant presence in early medieval Britain.

The sustained presence of Frisians in early medieval Britain also offers us a chance to expand our understanding of multilingual marriages among non-elites. The anonymous and undated Old English gnomic poem found in the *Exeter Book* and known as *Maxims I* includes a famous scene of a sailor welcomed home by his 'Frisian wife'. The relevant passage reads:

> The ship must be fastened with nails, the shield bound, the light linden board; and the beloved man (must be) welcome to the Frisian woman when his boat stands in; his ship has come and her husband as well to home, her own provider, and she invites him in, washes his dirty garments and gives him fresh clothes, lies with him on land as his love urges.[189]

This poetic passage extends the association between Frisians and seafaring seen elsewhere in the historical record of early medieval Britain. It also raises a fascinating question when considering the island's multilingual landscape, namely, does *Maxims I* depict a Frisian couple, or just a Frisian wife? If the latter, *Maxims I* is evidence for the reality of non-elite multilingual marriages in early medieval Britain. While such unions surely must have occurred, particularly in border regions such as the Anglo-Welsh or Anglo-Scottish borderlands and the Danelaw, *Maxims I* may offer us rare written evidence of the likely reality that many Frisians who settled in Anglo-Saxon England would have married locals. Yet even if *Maxims I* depicts a Frisian couple, its poignant image of a wife waiting for her husband to return from sea reminds us that Frisians were part of early medieval Britain, and examining the lives of traders shows how speakers from different linguistic backgrounds would have settled into their local communities. Personal names are also an important category of evidence for mobility and linguistic contact. When people from different

---

[188] Altfrid, *Vita Sancti Liudgeri*, ch. 12; trans. Whitelock, *English Historical Documents*, 840.
[189] *Maxims I*, ll. 93–99; trans. Howe, *Writing the Map of Anglo-Saxon England*, 54.

linguistic backgrounds settled in a new place, we often find personal names that reflect their 'foreign' identities. For instance, as Julia Crick has noted from the other direction, 'the names of more than a thousand migrants bearing names suggesting origin in England, Wales, and France are recorded as citizens of Dublin *c.* 1200'.[190]

Medieval Britain's trade networks expanded significantly during the Viking Age. One facet of the Vikings' success was their ship-building, and the Viking world was connected by water.[191] Consequently, the Viking Age ushered in a new era of expansive trade routes that linked together much of the known medieval world.[192] With this expanded network came increased opportunities for multilingual contact. A detailed case study of the importance of multilingualism to travel and trade is provided by the interpolations known as the *Voyages of Ohthere and Wulfstan* within the *Old English Orosius*. During the late ninth or early tenth century, almost certainly under the auspices of King Alfred's vernacular translation programme,[193] an anonymous Anglo-Saxon scholar (or group of scholars) translated the popular historical work known as the *Seven Books of History Against the Pagans* (*Historiarum Adversum Paganos Libri VII*)[194] by the early fifth-century cleric and scholar Orosius into Old English.[195] Embedded in the beginning of this work is some unique material: the accounts of two foreign travellers, Ohthere and Wulfstan, who reported their knowledge of the geography and cultures of the far north to an interested Anglo-Saxon audience at King Alfred's court.[196] The voyages of Ohthere and Wulfstan highlight the ways in which merchants and traders helped to spread knowledge as well as physical goods throughout the early medieval world. The narratives of these travellers paint a picture of men who were explorers and cultural anthropologists as much as they were traders. Their stories emphasise the centrality of multilingualism not only to their own adventures but also to those audiences, like that of King Alfred's court, with whom these tales were shared.

The accounts of Ohthere and Wulfstan embedded within the *Old English Orosius* represent moments of intellectual and multilingual exchange. The two

---

[190] Crick, '"The English" and "The Irish" from Cnut to John', 221; see her broader discussion for Irish names in Britain.

[191] Cooijmans, *Monarchs and Hydrarchs*.

[192] Gruszczyński, Jankowiak, and Shepard, *Viking-Age Trade*; Jarman, *River Kings*; Horne, *A Viking Market Kingdom in Ireland and Britain*.

[193] Bately, 'The Old English Orosius'.

[194] Fear, *Orosius: Seven Books of History against the Pagans*.

[195] Bately, *The Old English Orosius*.

[196] Lund and Fell, *Two Voyagers at the Court of King Alfred*; Bately and Englert, *Ohthere's Voyages*; Valtonen, *The North in the Old English Orosius*; Englert and Trakadas, *Wulfstan's Voyage*; Allport, 'Home Thoughts of Abroad'.

men are travellers, sharing information about their journeys and experiences with King Alfred's receptive court. The *Old English Orosius* records that: 'Ohthere told his lord King Alfred that he lived furthest north of all Northmen' and that 'Wulfstan reported that he traveled from Hedeby'.[197] Ohthere and Wulfstan were not reporting back to their own king, but rather, engaging in an exchange of information as visitors and guests. The two men would have spoken different languages from the members of Alfred's court – and indeed, most likely from one another – but their narratives were recorded for posterity in Old English. During the course of their visit, Ohthere and Wulfstan would also have received information about Anglo-Saxon England, which they would have brought home to their contemporaries in return. However, only half of the exchanges between these men and Alfred's court has been recorded in the *Old English Orosius*, presumably because the other half contained information that was already familiar to an Anglo-Saxon audience.[198] Yet from a multilingual perspective, it is clear that these two travellers were sharing information directly with Alfred's court, meaning either that they could speak Old English themselves or that there was an interpreter who spoke their language(s) present. The voyages of Ohthere and Wulfstan are a striking illustration of the wide geographic and linguistic range of travellers who passed through early medieval Britain.

The detailed accounts of their voyages also provide a good overview of the importance of multilingualism to travel and trade in the early medieval period. Discussing Ohthere's status in his own society, the Anglo-Saxon author notes that 'he was a very wealthy man in terms of the things that constitute their wealth, that is in wild animals . . . their wealth is mainly in the tax that the Sami pay them'.[199] His biographical details emphasise that communication across linguistic groups is fundamental to the accumulation of wealth in his culture. Yet Ohthere is not only a trader, but also an explorer: 'he said that on one occasion he decided to find out how far the country extended northward, or whether anyone lived to the north of that uninhabited region'.[200] He encountered many different peoples during the course of his travels, and it is clear that he was able to converse with them. For example, at one point in his narrative, Ohthere reported that 'the Biarmians told him lots of stories about their own country and about the territory around them, but he didn't know what the truth was since he hadn't seen it himself'.[201] He also seems keenly aware of

---

[197] Godden, *The Old English History of the World*, 36–7 and 44–5.
[198] Englert, 'Ohthere's Voyages as Seen from a Nautical Angle'.
[199] Godden, *The Old English History of the World*, 40–1.
[200] Godden, *The Old English History of the World*, 36–7.
[201] Godden, *The Old English History of the World*, 38–9.

similarities and differences in the languages of others, at one point stating that 'he thought that the Sami and the Biarmians spoke almost the same language'.[202] Ohthere's narrative underscores his status as a well-travelled and experienced trader who can communicate with peoples from across a wide range of geographic regions and linguistic groups – as those communities that he passed through could understand him in turn. The details of his journey emphasise not only how important it was for merchants and traders to be able to communicate with speakers of various languages, but also how commonplace this type of practical multilingualism was: at no point in Ohthere's narrative does the Anglo-Saxon author recording it comment on his linguistic abilities as unusual or exceptional, nor do the peoples that Ohthere encountered on his voyage express surprise at his presence. Ohthere's account reminds us that even those who did not travel themselves would have had many opportunities to encounter visitors, and consequently speakers of other languages, passing through their communities. The narratives of travellers like Ohthere are also valuable records of the names of the places and peoples he encountered, names which help modern scholars to understand the linguistic relationships that existed within these regions.[203]

Wulfstan's account contains fewer explicit references to multilingualism, but its implicit frequency and utility during travel and trade are no less significant of a thread within his narrative, which records his experiences travelling around the eastern Baltic Sea region. Like Ohthere, he is unproblematically welcomed by the communities he encounters, and most of his account is devoted to describing the homeland and culture of a people whom he refers to as the Ests. In particular, Wulfstan provides a detailed narrative of Est funeral customs, based on what appears to be his own eyewitness accounts and participation in an Est funeral. Every detail in Wulfstan's narrative suggests that he lived among the Ests for a fairly sustained period of time. For example, he notes that a key part of Estish funeral customs is hospitality to strangers. After someone dies, he reports, the Ests 'dispose of almost all his property through the long lying-in at the dead persons's house and by what they lay out along the road, which strangers ride to and take'.[204] He also calls attention to the protracted length of funerals among the Ests, stating that: 'There is a custom among the Ests that when anyone dies, the body lies in his house uncremated, with his family and friends, for a month or two. The kings and the other leading people sometimes lie uncremated for half a year and remain above ground in their houses, the more wealth they have the longer

---

[202] Godden, *The Old English History of the World*, 38–9.
[203] Valtonen, *The North in the Old English Orosius*.
[204] Godden, *The Old English History of the World*, 46–7.

they lie there'.[205] Wulfstan's account conveys the impression of a man who was not just an observer of, but an active participant in, the cultures of the societies he travelled through. It is clear that the events of his narrative could not have transpired as recorded if he could not communicate with the peoples among whom he was travelling.

Of course, not all travellers were interested in trade. Sadly, we do not have any surviving ethnographic accounts of travel around Britain – in the style of the tenth-century Arabic diplomat Ahmad ibn Fadlan's narrative of his travels among the Rus' – until later in the period, when Gerald of Wales wrote his *Journey through Wales* and *Description of Wales* in the late twelfth century. However, some light can be shed on the types of multilingual situations that travellers to early medieval Britain would have encountered by depictions of such journeys in a subgroup of Icelandic sagas known as *Íslendingasögur* (*Sagas of Icelanders* or *Family Sagas*) set during the ninth to eleventh centuries. These vernacular prose narratives must be treated with caution as historical sources for the Viking Age, as they were written hundreds of years later, from the thirteenth century onwards, after the Christianisation of Iceland in the year 1000 caused a significant increase in literacy and the use of durable written records among the Vikings' descendants, who then began to write down stories about their ancestors. Nonetheless, those episodes scattered throughout the *Íslendingasögur* of Vikings' journeys to Britain provide useful illustrations of the range of situations, challenges, and opportunities that the intersection of multiple languages in early medieval Britain was perceived to provide.

Britain – and indeed, anywhere 'abroad' from Iceland – was largely depicted in the *Sagas of Icelanders* as a place of opportunity where men could seek their fortunes. Opportunities could come in many forms, and it is unsurprising to find that 'going Viking' (raiding) around Britain is one of the most commonly-depicted ways in which Icelanders in the sagas are seen to acquire wealth. Raiding itself was not depicted as a particularly multilingual activity, but other opportunities were. In particular, the sagas commonly portray Icelanders as having earned their fortunes in Britain by fighting as mercenaries for a foreign king, participating in Anglo-Saxon court culture and being rewarded for poetry or loyalty, or trading with insular merchants. Each of these scenarios involved a high level of multilingual interaction. A few examples from the sagas illustrate the range of multilingual scenarios that travellers to early medieval Britain could have encountered, including their pitfalls and opportunities.

The sagas depict the early medieval insular world as a place where a young man could make his fortune and reputation fighting as a mercenary for a foreign

---

[205] Godden, *The Old English History of the World*, 44–7.

king. *Egils saga*, which describes events beginning in the late ninth century but was written in the thirteenth, provides a good illustration of this pattern in early medieval Britain; the contemporary *Njáls saga* is a good example of the same types of events in an Irish setting, as its conclusion depicts a significant Icelandic contingent fighting in the early eleventh-century Battle of Clontarf. In *Egils saga*, during the tenth-century reign of King Æthelstan, the king promised 'rewards to all who joined and were looking for money, whether they came from home or abroad'.[206] The central saga character Egil and his brother Thorolf 'learned that the King of England needed troops and the rewards were likely to be high. So they made up their minds to go, and travelled over autumn till they reached King Athelstan'.[207] After they arrived, the saga reports, the king 'gave them a good welcome and it seemed to him their support would be a great asset to his army. They hadn't been talking to him long before he made them an offer to guard his frontiers, whereupon terms were agreed to and they became Athelstan's men'.[208] This episode is set within the historical past but is by no means itself historically accurate,[209] and the odds that King Æthelstan personally extended a warm welcome to a handful of itinerant Icelandic mercenaries are exceedingly slender. Yet in *Egils saga*, as in the narratives of the *Voyages of Ohthere and Wulfstan*, there exists an assumption that speakers of other languages who travelled to Anglo-Saxon England would have been able to communicate without difficulty.

A further illustration of the perceived ease with which communication was possible for travellers in Anglo-Saxon England can be seen in *Egils saga's* description of a common practice known as 'primsigning'. As *Egils saga* explains the ritual: King Æthelstan 'asked Thorolf and his brother to accept preliminary baptism as was the custom in those days both for merchants and mercenaries serving Christian rulers, since people who had been given this form of baptism could mix equally with Christian and heathen and were free to hold any belief that suited them'.[210] Of particular interest to considerations of multilingualism is the fact that this passage mentions both merchants and mercenaries, underscoring some popular (and profitable) motives for travel during the Viking Age. Moreover, primsigning is depicted as a common custom in both the saga corpus and historical records from the Viking Age itself. Significantly, as in the case of Viking leader Guthrum's baptism, in order for primsigning to occur in any sort of theologically viable way, those who

---

[206] Pálsson and Edwards, *Egil's Saga*, ch. 50, 116.

[207] Pálsson and Edwards, *Egil's Saga*, ch. 50, 116.

[208] Pálsson and Edwards, *Egil's Saga*, ch. 50, 116.

[209] Fjalldal, *Anglo-Saxon England in Icelandic Medieval Texts*.

[210] Pálsson and Edwards, *Egil's Saga*, ch. 50, 116.

underwent the ritual must have been able to understand what was taking place themselves or to rely upon the presence of interpreters to translate the proceedings for them.

Egils saga also contains a number of scenes reflecting the intersection of multilingual activity and court culture in early medieval Britain. After a major battle in which Æthelstan's army is victorious but Egil's brother Thorolf is killed (due in large part to the king's bad tactical advice), Æthelstan holds a feast at which Egil demonstrates visible grief until the king properly compensates him for his brother's death. During these events, Egil composes and recites several poems in Old Norse verse of varying degrees of difficulty. No mention is made of an interpreter, but Æthelstan is depicted as having understood and appreciated the content of Egil's poetry. Multilingual court culture is also illustrated later in the saga, in a famous episode in which a shipwrecked Egil washes up in Northumbria at the court of his old enemy Eirik Bloodaxe and must compose a praise-poem to the king – literally entitled *Höfuðlausn* (head-ransom) – in the difficult *drápa* verse in order to save his life. While Eirik, who speaks the same native language as Egil, has no difficulty understanding the latter's *drápa*, the fact that this episode takes place in Northumbria reminds us that a significant proportion of the 'court culture' of Britain during the late Anglo-Saxon period was in fact Norse-speaking.

The potential interpretive difficulties of performative skaldic poetry are raised by a group of sagas sometimes collectively known as the 'sagas of warrior-poets'. In one example of this genre, *Gunnlaugs saga ormstungu* (the *Saga of Gunnlaug Serpent-Tongue*), the eponymous Gunnlaug travels around various early medieval kingdoms in order to perform his craft. He is not received well in Norway due to his difficult character (a common theme in the warrior-poets' sagas), but his visits to Anglo-Saxon England and Ireland are of particular interest from a multilingual perspective. Before Gunnlaug arrives in Britain, the saga sets the scene by informing its audience that 'in those days, the language in England was the same as that spoken in Norway and Denmark, but there was a change of language when William the Bastard conquered England':[211] a statement which is 'exaggerated but not wholly false'.[212] It is particularly noteworthy that the saga-author stresses the intelligibility of Gunnlaug's poetry to an Anglo-Saxon audience given the events that follow in Ireland. Gunnlaug appears before the Anglo-Saxon king (Æthelred 'the unready' in this case), recites his poem, which the king appreciates, and is duly rewarded with an expensive cloak and a position in the king's retinue. After

---

[211] Attwood, *Saga of Gunnlaug Serpent-tongue*, ch. 7, 240.

[212] Attwood, *Saga of Gunnlaug Serpent-tongue*, 459 n. 17.

the winter season, Gunnlaug continues to Ireland, where he arrives in Dublin to again perform his poetry, this time at the court of king Sigtrygg Silkbeard. Sigtrygg, as the saga emphasises, is a Hiberno-Norse ruler; son of the (Viking) father Olaf Cuarán and (Irish) mother Gormflaith ingen Murchada. When Gunnlaug presents himself to Sigtrygg, the king responds: 'No one has ever deigned to bring me a poem before. Of course I will listen to it'.[213] After Gunnlaug recites his poem, Sigtrygg's treasurer must dissuade him from rewarding Gunnlaug with two ships, and manages to talk him down to a new scarlet suit, an embroidered tunic, a fur cloak, and a gold bracelet. It is unclear what precisely *Gunnlaugs saga* is implying in this exchange: That Viking-Age Dublin was a cultural backwater where so few poets visited that its kings had no idea how to reward them properly? That Sigtrygg's half-Irish ancestry somehow played a role in his not understanding Gunnlaug's poem or the customs surrounding its recital? That Sigtrygg himself was a bumpkin who was too easily dazzled? Regardless of the precise target of this saga's satire, Gunnlaug's poetic adventures serve as a vivid illustration of the multilingual nature of kings' courts during the Viking era and of the frequent visitors to them who were travelling for purely cultural purposes.

Finally, a significant portion of travel to Britain during the Viking Age involved trade. In order for trade to be carried out successfully, speakers of different languages must have been able to communicate with one another. An illustration of the practical linguistic difficulties that could arise during trade is provided by *Laxdæla saga*. A key part of this saga's early plot centres around the figure of Melkorka, an Irish princess captured in a slave raid and eventually sold to an Icelander named Hoskuld, who rapes her and brings her back to Iceland as his concubine. Melkorka gives birth to a son, Olaf, to whom she teaches her native Irish language. She eventually reveals that her father, Myrkjartan, was an Irish king, and when Olaf reaches adulthood he sets off to Ireland to prove his ancestry and reclaim his mother's honour. During the voyage, Olaf's ship hits a bad patch of fog and becomes stranded off the Irish coast. One of his companions laments:

> I'm afraid we won't be well received. We're far from any port or merchant town where foreigners are assured of trading in peace, and now the tide has gone out and left us stranded here like a minnow. It's my guess that, according to Irish law, they'll lay claim to all the property we have on board; they call it a stranded ship when less than this has ebbed from the stern of the ship.[214]

---

[213] Attwood, *Saga of Gunnlaug Serpent-tongue*, ch. 8, 245.
[214] Kunz, *Saga of the People of Laxardal*, 39.

His gloomy predictions nonetheless underscore his familiarity with Irish salvage law, a familiarity which he could have only gained through his own
multilingual ability or contact with someone else who had it. However, the
fortunes of these particular travellers are saved by the knowledge of the Irish
language and of Irish law that Olaf's mother had taught him. Once their ship has
been properly stranded, Irish crowds approach from the shore. They interrogate
the Icelanders, and:

> Olaf replied to them in Irish, as they had spoken in that tongue. When the Irish
> learned that they were Norse, they referred to their laws on ship strandings
> and said that if the ship's company handed over all the property on board they
> would be unharmed until the king had pronounced his judgment in their case.
> Olaf said that this was indeed the law if there was no interpreter among the
> traders.[215]

This episode underscores the value and utility that multilingualism was perceived to hold in the early medieval period. While this particular interlude in
Laxdæla saga is set in Ireland, and the nuances of salvage law would have
differed in Britain, its central message is equally applicable to both regions.
Knowledge of multiple languages was a valuable commodity that increased
one's chances of fortune during travel and trade. And as we have seen in
discussions throughout this section, those travellers and traders who passed
through Britain also brought with them increased opportunities for contact with
speakers of multiple languages from across the early medieval world.

Conclusion: Multilingual Britain after the Norman Conquest of England

In the late eleventh century, Britain underwent a significant linguistic, cultural,
and political shift in the aftermath of the Norman Conquest of England.[216] The
Norman kingdom was formed in the early tenth century via a treaty between
Viking leader Rollo and Frankish king Charles the Simple that granted Frankish
lands to Rollo and his people after his public baptism and conversion to
Christianity. Normandy was defined in contemporary historical writing by its
combined Scandinavian and Frankish character, and the kingdom became an
increasingly important player in European politics over the course of the tenth
and eleventh centuries.[217] At the Battle of Hastings on 14 October 1066, Harold
Godwinson, the last Anglo-Saxon king, was defeated and killed by William,

---

[215] Kunz, *Saga of the People of Laxardal*, 40.
[216] Williams, *The English and the Norman Conquest*; Thomas, *The Norman Conquest*; Faith, *The Moral Economy of the Countryside*.
[217] Chibnall, *The Normans*.

Duke of Normandy (later known as William the Conqueror), who was subsequently crowned king of England.

The Norman Conquest of England was understood as a watershed moment at the time it took place. A poem in the *Peterborough Chronicle* (a post-Conquest continuation of the *Anglo-Saxon Chronicle*) in the annal for 1087 eulogises William in a way that makes the perceived impact of the Conquest clear. The poem, known as the *Rime of King William*, begins: 'Castelas he let wyrcean, / 7 earme men swiðe swencean. / Se cyng wæs swa swiðe stearc, / 7 benam of his underþeoddan manig marc / goldes 7 ma hundred punda seolfres' (He had castles built, and miserable men worked hard. The king was very harsh, and he took from his subjects many marks of gold and further hundreds of pounds of silver).[218] In the aftermath of the Conquest, William had undertaken a comprehensive survey of England, known as the Domesday Book, for taxation purposes. The Domesday Book itself contains valuable linguistic evidence of Old English placenames in their eleventh-century forms, but the process of compiling these records was viewed as an imposition, wherein 'so very narrowly did [William] have [the land] investigated, that there was no single hide nor virgate of land, nor indeed (it is a shame to relate but it seemed no shame to him to do) one ox nor one cow nor one pig which was there left out, and not put down in his record'.[219] While the extent to which the Conquest actually impacted the life of an 'average' Anglo-Saxon has been debated,[220] it is clear that William's reign was perceived as an immediate and oppressive shift in government: literally so, as the *Rime of King William*'s first line refers to the hundreds of motte-and-bailey castles built in the twenty years following the Battle of Hastings, which marked the Conquest on the landscape of Britain in a very visible way.

In addition to its political consequences, the Norman Conquest also had a significant impact on the development of the English language.[221] The daily language of commerce, government, and politics gradually became Norman French. It would eventually develop into its own dialect, known as Anglo-Norman. Its grammatical, syntactical, and orthographic impact on Old English was substantial enough that the structure of the language itself changed, entering a new historical-linguistic phase known as Middle English. The linguistic impact of the Conquest extended to literary form: the *Rime of King William* is notable precisely for its use of tail rhyme, where most earlier Old English poetry

---

[218] Irvine, *Volume 7: MS. E*, s.a. 1086; Jurasinski, 'The *Rime of King William* and Its Analogues'.

[219] *Peterborough Chronicle* s.a. 1085; trans. Douglas and Greenaway, *English Historical Documents 1042–1189*, 160.

[220] Chibnall, *The Debate on the Norman Conquest*.

[221] Ingham, *The Transmission of Anglo-Norman*.

had been defined by alliteration.[222] Because these new linguistic developments were ushered in by the new rulers of Britain, there was a significant class dimension to the impact of the Norman Conquest on the English language. We can see this illustrated in the way that Old Norse borrowings into Old English have become 'homely' words in modern English, showing settlers of the Danelaw living side-by-side with their Anglo-Saxon neighbours; however, their Norman French equivalents have come to signify upper-class versions of the same concepts: consider such Old Norse/Norman French-derived pairs as kid/heir; stench/odour; egg/omelet; yard/court; skirt/costume; anger/cruelty; fight/battle; law/parliament; and knife/armour.

Those who lived through the Norman Conquest of England were well aware that it had caused significant changes to many facets of life, including to Britain's linguistic landscape. This Element began its survey of multilingualism in early medieval Britain by examining the importance of translations from Latin into the vernacular during the conversion era. At the end of the Anglo-Saxon period, the situation had in many ways been reversed. In a preface to his Latin *Deeds* of the Anglo-Saxon outlaw and rebel against William the Conqueror known as Hereward the Wake, the anonymous author explains that he has translated English accounts of Hereward's life into Latin to preserve what was already in the process of being lost. His biography of Hereward was 'translated into Latin, with the addition of things we happened to hear from our own people with whom he was familiar', because men used to 'collect together from histories or from trustworthy stories all the exploits of great heroes and fighters of ancient times' and 'for their remembrance to commit them to writing in English', but when our author sought out such tales concerning Hereward, he 'found nothing complete – only a few loose pages, partly rotten with damp and decayed and partly damaged by tearing'.[223] The preface to the *Deeds* of Hereward the Wake offers a lament for the state of vernacular learning in the aftermath of the Norman Conquest of England. And indeed, one narrative of multilingualism in post-Conquest Britain has focused on similar moments of loss and decay. For instance, the text known as the *Quadripartitus* was written in the early twelfth century (*c.* 1100), during the reign of Henry I. It combines Latin translations of Old English legal texts with a document recording the laws of Henry I, known as the *Leges Henrici Primi*. The *Quadripartitus* is an important work because it preserves the contents of several legal documents from the Anglo-Saxon period which do not survive independently, but to many scholars, it has suggested a narrative of vernacular loss similar to that

---

[222] McKie, 'The Origins and Early Development of Rhyme in English Verse'.
[223] Swanton, 'The Deeds of Hereward'.

lamented in the *Deeds* of Hereward the Wake, in which eleventh- and twelfth-century scholars raced to collect Old English material and translate it into Latin before the knowledge of how to read England's vernacular tongue died out forever.

Yet learning in the vernacular did not vanish; it evolved. A vibrant multilingual culture persisted in post-Norman England, but it now included French alongside Middle English and Latin, while Welsh, Cornish, Scottish Gaelic, and eventually Scots were spoken in other regions of Britain. In the pre-Norman period, we have seen contemporary recognition of Britain's multilingual landscape by figures such as Bede and the author of the *Historia Brittonum*. The same awareness was demonstrated in the post-Norman period by intellectuals such as twelfth-century author Gerald of Wales, who in his *Itinerarium Cambriae* ('Journey through Wales') related the story of a man who was said to have encountered a race of 'little folk' as a child. As evidence of the tale's veracity, Gerald reported that the man could still remember some words of their language, which was 'very like Greek'. In an erudite discussion, Gerald went on to illustrate lexical parallels between several Indo-European languages – Greek, Latin, Welsh, Irish, French, English, and German – by comparing their words for 'water' and 'salt'. He even provided a pseudohistorical explanation for these linguistic connections, writing that 'the Britons stayed a long time in Greece after the fall of Troy and then took their name from their leader Brutus, so that the early Welsh language (*lingua Britannica*) is similar to Greek in many of its details'.[224] In the post-Norman period as well, then, those living in Britain understood it to be an inherently multilingual space.

It used to be believed that the linguistic climate of post-Norman England was trilingual, but striated, with French the language of bureaucracy and aristocracy, Latin the language of religion and learning, and English (or other vernaculars) the language of the peasantry. We have already seen that the situation was more complex in our investigation of the preface to the *Deeds* of Hereward the Wake, which describes a persistent, if waning, vernacular intellectual culture in post-Conquest England, and studies on the 'French of England' have also rejected the idea that the linguistic landscape of post-Norman Britain was rigidly stratified in three discrete strands.[225] Another illustration of this linguistic complexity can be found in the French names widespread among the children of Anglo-Saxon families born in the generations after the Conquest, to the extent that it would be 'unsafe to assume that a French name after the middle of the twelfth century implies French ancestry'.[226] From the frequency of

[224] Thorpe, *Gerald of Wales: The Journey through Wales and the Description of Wales*, 135–6.
[225] Wogan-Browne, 'What's in a Name: The "French" of "England"'.
[226] Sawyer, *From Roman Britain to Norman England*, 257.

multilingual texts and manuscripts, to the language used in letters and legal petitions, to that spoken in court and in small towns, by communities ranging from nuns to sailors, it is clear that multilingualism was just as prevalent in post-Norman as in pre-Norman Britain.

But what did Britain's multilingual culture look like, practically speaking, after the events of 1066? This brief conclusion will survey a few illustrative case studies. Section 1's investigation of multilingual texts and manuscripts from the early medieval period discussed some macaronic texts which were carefully composed to flaunt their authors' knowledge of multiple languages. Such works were no less popular in the post-Conquest period; they simply came to encompass French as well. A good example of the creativity that this genre could inspire is demonstrated by a pair of trilingual macaronic poems, written in the form of two letters exchanged between lovers, whose rhyme scheme makes use of French, English, and Latin, combined in that order. Ad Putter has contextualised their composition in light of later medieval England's trilingual intellectual and cultural milieu.[227] In the sample stanzas from each poem below, we can see that multilingualism is inherent to their structure and meaning:

A celuy que plus eyme en mounde,	*To the one whom I most love in the world*
Of alle tho that I have found[e]	
Carissima,	*Dearest*
Saluz od treyé amour	*Greetings with faithful love*
With grace and joye and alle honour	
Dulcissima.	*Sweetest (lady)*
De moy, jeo pry, aves pyté,	*On me, I beg, have pity*
I falle so doth the lef on tre	
Tristando;	*With grieving*
Tot le mounde, longe et lé	*All the world far and wide*
I woldë leve and takë thee	
Zelando.	*With fervour*[228]

These poems have 'a much more sophisticated design' than some contemporary macaronic works because 'the audience who read, or more likely heard, this for the first time would have every reason to expect a redundant tag in the Latin, since the sense of the French and English lines is apparently complete'; however, 'the Latin tricks us with an unexpected layer of grammatical complexity'.[229] All three

---

[227] Putter, 'Two Trilingual Verse Epistles'.

[228] *De amico*, 1–6 and *Responcio*, 25–30; ed. and trans. Putter, 'Two Trilingual Verse Epistles', 399 and 400.

[229] Putter, 'Two Trilingual Verse Epistles', 400 and 402.

languages work together to complete the poems' lines, meaning that a knowledge of all three was required in order to fully understand these texts. The cultural milieu which underlay the composition of works such as these mirrors the traditional understanding of the post-Conquest linguistic landscape in some ways: English was the language of vernacular communication, French the language of letters, and Latin the language of religion and education. However, knowledge of these languages is no longer understood as isolated or restricted. This pair of trilingual macaronic love poems demonstrates that their author was familiar with each of later medieval England's three distinctive linguistic milieux and was able to successfully combine these divergent registers into something holistic, complex, and beautiful.

The trilingual cultural and intellectual milieu of later medieval England can also be seen in multilingual manuscripts,[230] such as the collection often referred to as the *Harley Lyrics* (London, British Library MS Harley 2253),[231] a manuscript containing items in French, English, and Latin as well as macaronic works that combine these languages. Harley 2253 contains an impressive range of texts including secular love lyrics, contemporary political songs, religious poems, four fabliaux, three lives of Anglo-Saxon saints, and 'a wealth of satires, comedies, debates, interludes, collected sayings, conduct literature, Bible stories, dream interpretations, and pilgrim guides'.[232] The manuscript as it stands was compiled by a single scribe, known as the Ludlow scribe, who 'worked fluently in three languages'.[233] While we do not know precisely for whom this manuscript was compiled or commissioned, Harley 2253 makes clear that both the appetite for and the ability to read a range of textual genres and forms across three languages underpinned the cultural and intellectual landscape of post-Conquest Britain.

French, English, and Latin were not the only languages in use throughout Britain after the Conquest. In Wales, the narrative of post-Conquest vernacular decay and decline is contradicted by a group of texts often collectively referred to as the *Brutiau*.[234] During the first half of the twelfth century, a cleric called Geoffrey of Monmouth wrote a wildly popular pseudohistorical work known as *De gestis Britonum* ('On the Deeds of the Britons', also referred to as the *Historia regum Britanniae*, 'The History of the Kings of Britain'). *De gestis Britonum* is best-known as the source via which the legend of King Arthur

[230] Scahill, 'Trilingualism in Early Middle English Miscellanies'.

[231] Fein, *Studies in the Harley Manuscript*; Fein, Raybin and Ziolkowski, *The Complete Harley 2253 Manuscript*, vols. 1–3.

[232] Fein, 'Introduction', *The Complete Harley 2253 Manuscript*, vol. 1.

[233] Fein, 'Introduction', *The Complete Harley 2253 Manuscript*, vol. 1.

[234] Jones, *Historical Writing in Medieval Wales*; Pryce, *Writing Welsh History*.

exploded into the literary landscape of high medieval Europe. However, Geoffrey's text was also a significant factor in the writing of Welsh history in the vernacular from the twelfth century onwards, because it was considered part of 'a Welsh tradition of historical writing'.[235] The appearance of *De gestis Britonum* sparked a flurry of translations and continuations of Geoffrey's narrative into the vernacular in later medieval Wales. These texts used *De gestis Britonum* as the source for the history of Wales in the early medieval period, from which the historical narrative was extended into the present moment by vernacular annals and chronicles. The vernacular translations and expansions of *De gestis Britonum* are reflective of contemporary trends in Welsh literary tradition, which saw an increase of vernacular writing more broadly, much of which encompassed translations of a range of Latin texts.[236] Welsh historical writing in the high medieval period was prolific, comprised of numerous complex and interrelated strands, all of which were widely circulated.[237] Together, these texts reveal the existence of a multilingual literary culture in which Latin works served as the basis for vernacular translation and inspiration, and vice versa; producing a vibrant tradition of historical writing in high medieval Wales.

I want to close by considering a text that encapsulates nearly every literary language of post-Conquest southern Britain, namely, the fourteenth-century Anglo-Norman prose romance known as *Fouke le Fitz Waryn*. *Fouke*, often referred to by scholars as a 'border romance' or 'outlaw romance', would at first blush appear to possess no multilingual features at all, as it is written in Anglo-Norman. However, this sole surviving copy of *Fouke* in its Anglo-Norman prose format is actually one of several versions of this romance, written across multiple languages, which existed in later medieval Britain. The Anglo-Norman prose *Fouke* was derived from an earlier, now-lost, Anglo-Norman verse romance of the same legend. An also-lost Middle English variant of this romance in alliterative verse survived until the sixteenth century, when it was viewed by the antiquarian John Leland, who recorded evidence of many medieval texts and manuscripts destroyed during the dissolution of the monasteries. Ralph Hanna has characterised the surviving text of *Fouke* as a Marcher romance, 'one responsive to a cultural milieu that is Welsh as well as Angevin', and Joshua Byron Smith has suggested that a Welsh-language version of this legend existed as well.[238] *Fouke le Fitz Waryn* describes the historical rebellion of thirteenth-century Marcher lord Fulk FitzWarin III against King John in an ahistorical romance narrative. Though Fulk and other Marcher lords are often

---

[235] Pryce, *Writing Welsh History*, 52.   [236] Pryce, *Writing Welsh History*.
[237] Jones, 'Geoffrey of Monmouth and Medieval Welsh Historical Writing'.
[238] Hanna, 'The Matter of Fulk', 342; Smith, 'Fouke le Fitz Waryn', 295.

characterised as Anglo-Norman, the perspective of this romance, and that of many other texts produced in the Welsh Marches, as Georgia Henley has convincingly demonstrated, is deeply embedded within a Welsh cultural, literary, and historical milieu.[239] The sole surviving copy of *Fouke le Fitz Waryn*, moreover, was written by none other than the Ludlow scribe,[240] whom we have already seen as the compiler of the trilingual manuscript Harley 2253. To this we may well add a fourth: Ludlow is in Shropshire, in the Anglo-Welsh borderlands, and our scribe lived in the same Marcher lordship which belonged to the historical Fulk FitzWarin III and whose loss drove *Fouke*'s narrative of outlawry and rebellion against King John. The fortunate survival of texts such as *Fouke le Fitz Waryn* illustrates the vibrant multilingual culture of Britain after the Norman Conquest of England.

This Element has surveyed the multilingual nature of literary culture in early medieval Britain, as well as the ways in which languages and their speakers interacted on a daily basis. Multiple languages shaped the religious, intellectual, political, and cultural history of early medieval Britain, which remained a space through which speakers of these languages continued to pass after the events of 1066. Britain was an island, but it was not isolated, and its intellectual communities continued to produce and value multilingual texts and manuscripts from the post-Roman through the post-Norman periods. By discarding the nationalistic biases that too often surround vernacular 'literary traditions' in the early medieval period, we can arrive at a better understanding of the intellectual environments in which knowledge was produced and shared during this time.

---

[239] Henley, *Reimagining the Past in the Medieval Borderlands of England and Wales.*

[240] Henley, *Reimagining the Past in the Medieval Borderlands of England and Wales*, ch. 1.

Bibliography

Primary Sources

Altfrid, *Vita Sancti Liudgeri*, in Wilhelm Diekamp (ed.), *Die Vitae Sancti Liudgeri* (Münster, 1881).

Attwood, Katrina (trans.), *The Saga of Gunnlaug Serpent-Tongue*, in Diana Whaley (ed.), *Sagas of Warrior-Poets* (London: Penguin Books, 2002).

Bately, Janet (ed.), *The Old English Orosius*, Early English Text Society, S.S. 6 (London: Oxford University Press, 1980).

Bately, Janet and Anton Englert (eds.), *Ohthere's Voyages: A Late 9th-Century Account of Voyages along the Coasts of Norway and Denmark and Its Cultural Contexts* (Roskilde: Viking Ship Museum, 2007).

Bodleian Library MS. Auct. F. 4. 32 (University of Oxford), http://image.ox.ac .uk/show?collection=bodleian&manuscript=msauctf432.

Cain, Christopher M., 'Phonology and Meter in the Old English Macaronic Verses', *Studies in Philology* 98 (2001): 273–91.

Christiansen, Reidar Thorolf, 'The People of the North', *Lochlann: A Review of Celtic Studies* 2 (1962): 137–64.

Colgrave, Bertram (ed. and trans.), *Felix's Life of Saint Guthlac* (Cambridge: Cambridge University Press, 1956; repr. paperback 1985).

Colgrave, Bertram and R. A. B. Mynors (ed. and trans.), *Bede's Ecclesiastical History of the English People* (Oxford: Clarendon Press, 1969; repr. 2007).

Douglas, David C. and George W. Greenaway, *English Historical Documents 1042–1189*, 2nd ed. (1981; repr. London: Routledge, 2007).

Dumville, David and Simon Keynes (gen. eds.), *The Anglo-Saxon Chronicle: A Collaborative Edition* (Cambridge: D.S. Brewer, 1983).

Edwards, Nancy, *A Corpus of Early Medieval Inscribed Stones and Stone Sculptures in Wales*, vol. 2 (Cardiff: University of Wales Press, 2007).

Edwards, Nancy, *A Corpus of Early Medieval Inscribed Stones and Stone Sculptures in Wales*, vol. 3 (Cardiff: University of Wales Press, 2013).

Emanuel, Hywel D., *The Latin Texts of the Welsh Laws* (Cardiff: University of Wales Press, 1967).

Englert, Anton and Athena Trakadas (eds.), *Wulfstan's Voyage: The Baltic Sea Region in the Early Viking Age as Seen from Shipboard* (Roskilde: Viking Ship Museum, 2009).

Fear, A. T. (trans.), *Orosius: Seven Books of History against the Pagans* (Liverpool: Liverpool University Press, 2010).

Fein, Susanna (ed.), with David Raybin and Jan Ziolkowski, *The Complete Harley 2253 Manuscript*, vols. 1–3 (Kalamazoo: Medieval Institute, 2014–15).

Godden, Malcolm R. (ed. and trans.), *The Old English History of the World: An Anglo-Saxon Rewriting of Orosius* (Cambridge, MA: Harvard University Press, 2016).

Gwara, Scott (ed. and trans.), '*De raris fabulis*, "On Uncommon Tales": A Glossed Latin Colloquy-Text from a Tenth-Century Cornish Manuscript', Basic Texts for Brittonic History 4 (Cambridge: Department of Anglo-Saxon, Norse, and Celtic, 2004).

Hessels, J. H. (ed.), *An Eighth-Century Latin-Anglo-Saxon Glossary Preserved in the Library of Corpus Christi College, Cambridge (MS no. 144)* (Cambridge: Cambridge University Press, 1890).

Howlett, David, 'Two Irish Jokes', in Pádraic Moran and Immo Warntjes (eds.), *Early Medieval Ireland and Europe: Chronology, Contacts, Scholarship. A Festschrift for Dáibhí Ó Cróinín* (Turnhout: Brepols, 2015), 225–64.

Hunt, R. W., *Saint Dunstan's Classbook from Glastonbury: Codex Biblioth. Bodleianae Oxon. Auct. F.4./32* (Amsterdam: North-Holland, 1961).

Ireland, Colin A. (ed. and trans.), *Old Irish Wisdom Attributed to Aldfrith of Northumbria: An Edition of Bríathra Flainn Fhína maic Ossu* (Tempe: ACMRS, 1999).

Irvine, Susan (ed.), *Volume 7: MS. E of The Anglo-Saxon Chronicle: A Collaborative Edition* (Cambridge: D. S. Brewer, 2004).

Keynes, Simon and Michael Lapidge, *Alfred the Great: Asser's Life of King Alfred and Other Contemporary Sources* (London: Penguin, 1983).

Krapp, George Philip and Elliott Van Kirk Dobbie (eds.), *The Anglo-Saxon Poetic Records*, 6 vols. (New York: Columbia University Press, 1931–53).

Kunz, Keneva (trans.) and Bergljót S. Kristjánsdóttir (ed.), *The Saga of the People of Laxardal and Bolli Bollason's Tale* (London: Penguin Books, 2008).

Liebermann, Felix, *Die Gesetze der Angelsachsen*, 3 vols. (Halle: Niemeyer, 1903–16).

Lindsay, W. M. (ed.), *The Corpus Glossary* (Cambridge: Cambridge University Press, 1921).

Lund, Niels (ed.) and Christine E. Fell (trans.), with contributory essays by Ole Crumlin-Pedersen, P. H. Sawyer, and Christine E. Fell, *Two Voyagers at the Court of King Alfred: The Ventures of Ohthere and Wulfstan Together with the Description of Northern Europe from the Old English Orosius* (New York: William Sessions, 1984).

McDonough, Christopher J., *Warner of Rouen, Moriuht: A Norman Latin Poem from the Early Eleventh Century* (Toronto: PIMS, 1995).

Morris, John (ed. and trans.), *Nennius: British History and the Welsh Annals* (London: Phillimore, 1980).

O'Donnell, Daniel Paul, *Cædmon's Hymn: A Multimedia Study, Archive and Edition* (Cambridge: D. S. Brewer, 2005).

Pálsson, Hermann and Paul Edwards (trans.), *Egil's Saga* (Harmondsworth: Penguin Books, 1976; repr. 1986).

Putter, Ad, 'The French of English Letters: Two Trilingual Verse Epistles in Context', in Wogan-Browne et al. (eds.), *The French of England*, 397–408.

Redknap, Mark and John M. Lewis, *A Corpus of Early Medieval Inscribed Stones and Stone Sculptures in Wales*, vol. 1 (Cardiff: University of Wales Press, 2007).

Smith, Joshua Byron, 'Fouke le Fitz Waryn', in Jocelyn Wogan-Browne, Thelma Fenster, and Delbert W. Russell (eds.), *Vernacular Literary Theory from the French of Medieval England: Texts and Translations, c.1120–c.1450* (Woodbridge: Boydell & Brewer, 2016), 293–302.

Sparrow, Andrew, 'Nigel Farage: Parts of Britain Are "Like a Foreign Land"', *The Guardian* (28 February 2014), www.theguardian.com/politics/2014/feb/28/nigel-farage-ukip-immigration-speech.

Swanton, M. J., (ed. and trans.), *The Anglo-Saxon Chronicle* (London: J. M. Dent, 1996; repr. New York: Routledge, 1998).

Swanton, Michael (trans.), 'The Deeds of Hereward', in Thomas H. Ohlgren (ed.), *Medieval Outlaws: Twelve Tales in Modern English Translation*, revised and expanded edition (Anderson, SC: Parlor Press, 2005), 28–99.

Sweet, Henry (ed.), *King Alfred's West Saxon Version of Gregory's Pastoral Care*, 2 vols., EETS o.s. 45 (London, 1871–2).

Thorpe, Lewis (trans.), *Gerald of Wales: The Journey through Wales and the Description of Wales* (London: Penguin Books, 1978).

Vindolanda Tablets Online (University of Oxford), http://vindolanda.csad.ox.ac.uk/.

Whitelock, Dorothy, *English Historical Documents*, vol. 1, c.500–1042, 2nd ed.2n (1955; repr. London: Routledge, 1996).

Williams, Myriah, 'Cambridge Juvencus (MS Ff.4.42)', https://cudl.lib.cam.ac.uk/views/MS-FF-00004-00042/4.

Winterbottom, Michael (ed. and trans.), *Gildas: The Ruin of Britain and Other Works* (London: Phillimore, 1978).

Secondary Sources

Abrams, Lesley, 'Edward the Elder's Danelaw', in N. J. Higham and D. H. Hill (eds.), *Edward the Elder, 899–924* (London: Routledge, 2001), 128–43.

Aird, William M., 'Interpreting the King's Will: Multilingualism and the Role of Interpreters in Eleventh- and Twelfth-Century England', in Naruki Haruta, Yukio Arai, and David Roffe (eds.), *Approaches to History: Essays in Honour of Hirokazu Tsurushima* (Tokyo: Tosuishobou, 2022), 29–41.

Allport, Ben, 'Home Thoughts of Abroad: *Ohthere's Voyage* in Its Anglo-Saxon Context', *Early Medieval Europe* 28 (2020): 256–88.

Ball, Martin J. with James Fife (eds.), *The Celtic Languages* (Abingdon: Routledge, 1993).

Barnes, Michael P., *Runes: A Handbook* (Woodbridge: The Boydell Press, 2012).

Bately, Janet M., 'The Old English Orosius', in Nicole Guenther Discenza and Paul E. Szarmach (eds.), *A Companion to Alfred the Great* (Leiden: Brill, 2015), 313–43.

Bédoyère, Guy de la, *Roman Britain: A New History* (New York: Thames and Hudson, 2006).

Beechy, Tiffany, *The Poetics of Old English* (Aldershot: Ashgate, 2010; repr. Abingdon: Routledge, 2016).

Benham, Jenny, *Peacemaking in the Middle Ages: Principles and Practice* (Manchester: Manchester University Press, 2011).

Bergin, O. J., 'A Middle-Irish Fragment of Bede's Ecclesiastical History', in O. J. Bergin, R. I. Best, Kuno Meyer, and J. G. O'Keeffe (eds.), *Anecdota from Irish Manuscripts*, vol. 3 (Halle, 1910), 63–76.

Bowman, Alan K., *Life and Letters on the Roman Frontier: Vindolanda and Its People* (Abingdon: Routledge, 1994).

Boyle, Elizabeth, *History and Salvation in Medieval Ireland* (Abingdon: Routledge, 2021).

Brady, Lindy, 'The "Dark Welsh" as Slaves and Slave Traders in Exeter Book Riddles 52 and 72', *English Studies* 95 (2014): 235–55.

Brady, Lindy, *Writing the Welsh Borderlands in Anglo-Saxon England* (Manchester: Manchester University Press, 2017).

Brady, Lindy, *The Origin Legends of Early Medieval Britain and Ireland* (Cambridge: Cambridge University Press, 2022).

Brady, Lindy, 'The Fluidity of Borderlands', *Offa's Dyke Journal* 4 (2022): 3–15.

Bremmer, Rolf H. Jr., 'Frisians in Anglo-Saxon England: A Historical and Toponymical Investigation', in N. R. Århammar, W. T. Beetstra, Ph. H. Breuker, and J. J. Spahr van der Hoek (eds.), *Fryske Nammen* (Leeuwarden: Fryske Akademy, 1981), 45–94.

Brink, Stefan, 'Who Were the Vikings?', in Stefan Brink (ed.) in collaboration with Neil Price, *The Viking World* (Abingdon: Routledge, 2008), 4–7.

Bromberg, Eric I., 'Wales and the Mediaeval Slave Trade', *Speculum* 17 (1942): 263–9.

Bruce, Scott G., *Silence and Sign Language in Medieval Monasticism: The Cluniac Tradition c.900–1200* (Cambridge: Cambridge University Press, 2007).

Bullough, Donald A., *Alcuin: Achievement and Reputation* (Leiden: Brill, 2004).

Callander, David, *Dissonant Neighbours: Narrative Progress in Early Welsh and English Poetry* (Cardiff: University of Wales Press, 2019).

Carley, James P., 'Two Pre-conquest Manuscripts from Glastonbury Abbey', *Anglo-Saxon England* 16 (1987): 197–212.

Cessford, Craig, 'Exogamous Marriages between Anglo-Saxons and Britons in Seventh Century Northern Britain', *Anglo-Saxon Studies in Archaeology and History* 9 (1996): 49–52.

Chadwick, Nora K., 'Early Culture and Learning in North Wales', in Nora K. Chadwick, Kathleen Hughes, Christopher Brooke, and Kenneth Jackson (eds.), *Studies in the Early British Church* (Cambridge: Cambridge University Press, 1958), 29–120.

Charles, B. G., *Old Norse Relations with Wales* (Cardiff: University of Wales Press, 1934).

Charles-Edwards, T. M., *Wales and the Britons, 350–1064* (Oxford: Oxford University Press, 2013).

Chibnall, Marjorie, *The Debate on the Norman Conquest* (Manchester: Manchester University Press, 1999).

Chibnall, Marjorie, *The Normans* (Oxford: Blackwell, 2006).

Clancy, Thomas Owen, 'Scotland, the "Nennian" Recension of the *Historia Brittonum*, and the *Lebor Bretnach*', in Simon Taylor (ed.), *Kings, Clerics, and Chronicles in Scotland, 500–1297: Essays in Honour of Marjorie Ogilvie Anderson on the Occasion of her Ninetieth Birthday* (Dublin: Four Courts Press, 2000), 87–107.

Clarke, Michael and Máire Ní Mhaonaigh (eds.), *Medieval Multilingual Manuscripts: Case Studies from Ireland to Japan* (Berlin: Walter de Gruyter, 2022).

Coates, Richard and Andrew Breeze, with a contribution by David Horovitz, *Celtic Voices, English Places: Studies of the Celtic Impact on Place-Names in England* (Stamford: Shaun Tyas, 2000).

Conneller, Chantal, *The Mesolithic in Britain: Landscape and Society in Times of Change* (Abingdon: Routledge, 2022).

Cooijmans, Christian, *Monarchs and Hydrarchs: The Conceptual Development of Viking Activity across the Frankish Realm (c. 750–940)* (Abingdon: Routledge, 2021).

Crick, Julia, '"The English" and "The Irish" from Cnut to John: Speculations on a Linguistic Interface', in Tyler (ed.), *Conceptualizing Multilingualism in England*, 217–37.

Cunliffe, Barry, *The Ancient Celts*, 2nd ed. (Oxford: Oxford University Press, 2018).

Dales, Douglas, *Alcuin: His Life and Legacy* (Cambridge: James Clarke, 2012).

Da Rold, Orietta, 'Classbook of St. Dunstan', www.le.ac.uk/english/em1060to1220/mss/EM.Ox.Auct.F.4.32.htm.

Darvill, Timothy, *Prehistoric Britain*, 2nd ed. (Abingdon: Routledge, 2010).

Downham, Clare, *Viking Kings of Britain and Ireland: The Dynasty of Ívarr to A.D. 1014* (Edinburgh: Dunedin Academic Press, 2007).

Duffy, Séan, 'Ostmen, Irish and Welsh in the Eleventh Century', *Peritia* 9 (1995): 379–96.

Dumville, David N., 'Sub-Roman Britain: History and Legend', *History* 62 (1977): 173–92.

Dumville, David N., 'The Historical Value of the *Historia Brittonum*', *Arthurian Literature* 6 (1986): 1–26.

Edmonds, Fiona, *Gaelic Influence in the Northumbrian Kingdom: The Golden Age and the Viking Age* (Woodbridge: Boydell, 2019).

Edwards, Nancy, 'Early Medieval Wales: Material Evidence and Identity', *Studia Celtica* 51 (2017): 65–87.

Englert, Anton, 'Ohthere's Voyages as Seen from a Nautical Angle', in Bately and Englert (eds.), *Ohthere's Voyages*, 117–29.

Etchingham, Colmán, 'North Wales, Ireland and the Isles: The Insular Viking zone', *Peritia* 15 (2001): 145–87.

Faith, Rosamond, *The Moral Economy of the Countryside: Anglo-Saxon to Anglo-Norman England* (Cambridge: Cambridge University Press, 2020).

Faull, Margaret Lindsay, 'The Semantic Development of Old English Wealh', *Leeds Studies in English* NS 8 (1975): 20–44.

Fein, Susanna (ed.), *Studies in the Harley Manuscript: The Scribes, Contents, and Social Contexts of British Library MS Harley 2253* (Kalamazoo: Medieval Institute, 2000).

Fjalldal, Magnús, *Anglo-Saxon England in Icelandic Medieval Texts* (Toronto: University of Toronto Press, 2005).

Fleming, Robin, *Britain after Rome: The Fall and Rise, 400–1070* (London: Allen Lane, 2010).

Fleming, Robin, *The Material Fall of Roman Britain, 300–525 CE* (Philadelphia: University of Pennsylvania Press, 2021).

Fordham, Michael, 'Peacekeeping and Order on the Anglo-Welsh Frontier in the Early Tenth Century', *Midland History* 32 (2007): 1–18.

Forsyth, Katherine, *Language in Pictland: The Case against 'Non-Indo-European Pictish'*, Studia Hameliana 2 (Utrecht: De Keltische Draak, 1997).

Forsyth, Katherine, 'Literacy in Pictland' in Huw Pryce (ed.), *Literacy in Medieval Celtic Societies* (Cambridge: Cambridge University Press, 1998), 39–61.

Frank, Roberta, 'King Cnut in the Verse of His Skalds', in Alexander R. Rumble (ed.), *The Reign of Cnut: King of England, Denmark and Norway* (London: Leicester University Press, 1994), 106–24.

Fraser, James E., *From Caledonia to Pictland: Scotland to 795* (Edinburgh: Edinburgh University Press, 2009).

Gallagher, Robert, Edward Roberts, and Francesca Tinti (eds.), *The Languages of Early Medieval Charters: Latin, Germanic Vernaculars, and the Written Word* (Leiden: Brill, 2021).

Geary, Patrick J., *The Myth of Nations: The Medieval Origins of Europe* (Princeton: Princeton University Press, 2002).

Gelling, Margaret, *The West Midlands in the Early Middle Ages* (Leicester: Leicester University Press, 1992), 112–19.

Gerrard, James, *The Ruin of Roman Britain: An Archaeological Perspective* (Cambridge: Cambridge University Press, 2013).

Gneuss, Helmut, 'A Grammarian's Greek-Latin Glossary in Anglo-Saxon England', in Malcolm Godden, Douglas Gray, and Terry Hoad (eds.), *From Anglo-Saxon to Early Middle English: Studies Presented to E. G. Stanley* (Oxford: Clarendon Press, 1994), 60–86.

Gransden, Antonia, 'Bede's Reputation as an Historian in Medieval England', *Journal of Ecclesiastical History* 32 (1981): 397–425.

Gretzinger, Joscha, et al., 'The Anglo-Saxon Migration and the Formation of the Early English Gene Pool', *Nature* 610 (2022): 112–19.

Grimmer, Martin, 'Britons in Early Wessex: The Evidence of the Law Code of Ine', in Higham (ed.), *Britons in Anglo-Saxon England*, 102–14.

Grimmer, Martin, 'The Exogamous Marriages of Oswiu of Northumbria', *The Heroic Age* 9 (2006), unpaginated online journal.

Gruszczyński, Jacek, Marek Jankowiak, and Jonathan Shepard (eds.), *Viking-Age Trade: Silver, Slaves and Gotland* (Abingdon: Routledge, 2021).

Guy, Ben, 'The Origins of the Compilation of Welsh Historical Texts in Harley 3859', *Studia Celtica* 49 (2015): 21–56.

Gwara, Scott, *Education in Wales and Cornwall in the Ninth and Tenth Centuries: Understanding De raris fabulis*, Kathleen Hughes Memorial Lectures on Mediaeval Welsh History 4 (Cambridge: Department of Anglo-Saxon, Norse, and Celtic, 2004).

Hadley, D. M., *The Northern Danelaw: Its Social Structure, c.800–1100* (London: Leicester University Press, 2000).

Han, Huamei, 'Trade Migration and Language', in Suresh Canagarajah (ed.), *The Routledge Handbook of Migration and Language* (Abingdon: Routledge, 2017), 258–74.

Hanna, Ralph, 'The Matter of Fulk: Romance and History in the Marches', *Journal of English and Germanic Philology* 110 (2011): 337–58.

Harding, D. W., *The Archaeology of Celtic Art* (Abingdon: Routledge, 2007).

Haselgrove, Colin and Tom Moore (eds.), *The Later Iron Age in Britain and beyond* (Oxford: Oxbow Books, 2007).

Haselgrove, Colin and Rachel Pope (eds.), *The Earlier Iron Age in Britain and the Near Continent* (Oxford: Oxbow Books, 2007).

Hayward, Paul, 'St Dunstan's Classbook', www.lancaster.ac.uk/staff/hay wardp/hist424/seminars/Auct_F.4.32.htm.

Helgason, Agnar, et al., 'mtDNA and the Origin of the Icelanders: Deciphering Signals of Recent Population History', *American Journal of Human Genetics* 66 (2000): 999–1016.

Helgason, Agnar, et al., 'Estimating Scandinavian and Gaelic Ancestry in the Male Settlers of Iceland', *American Journal of Human Genetics* 67 (2000): 697–717.

Helgason, Agnar, et al., 'mtDNA and the Islands of the North Atlantic: Estimating the Proportions of Norse and Gaelic Ancestry', *American Journal of Human Genetics* 68 (2001): 723–37.

Henley, Georgia, *Reimagining the Past in the Medieval Borderlands of England and Wales* (Oxford: Oxford University Press, 2024).

Higgit, John, Katherine Forsyth, and David N. Parsons (eds.), *Roman, Runes and Ogham: Medieval Inscriptions in the Insular World and on the Continent* (Donington: Shaun Tyas, 2001).

Higham, N. J. (ed.), *Britons in Anglo-Saxon England* (Woodbridge: Boydell, 2007).

Higley, Sarah Lynn, *Between Languages: The Uncooperative Text in Early Welsh and Old English Nature Poetry* (University Park: Pennsylvania State University Press, 1993).

Hines, John, 'Who Did the Anglo-Saxons Think They Were?', *Current Archaeology* 366 (2021).

Hines, John and Nelleke IJssennagger-van der Pluijm (eds.), *Frisians of the Early Middle Ages* (Woodbridge: The Boydell Press, 2021).

Holm, Poul, 'The Slave Trade of Dublin, Ninth to Twelfth Centuries', *Peritia* 5 (1986): 317–45.

Horne, Tom, *A Viking Market Kingdom in Ireland and Britain: Trade Networks and the Importation of a Southern Scandinavian Silver Bullion Economy* (Abingdon: Routledge, 2022).

Howe, Nicholas, *Writing the Map of Anglo-Saxon England: Essays in Cultural Geography* (New Haven: Yale University Press, 2008).

IJssennagger-van der Pluijm, Nelleke, 'Structured by the Sea: Rethinking Maritime Connectivity of the Early-Medieval Frisians', in Hines and IJssennagger-van der Pluijm (eds.), *Frisians of the Early Middle Ages*, 249–71.

Ingham, Richard, *The Transmission of Anglo-Norman: Language History and Language Acquisition* (Amsterdam: John Benjamins, 2012).

Insley, Charles, 'Languages of Boundaries and Boundaries of Language in Cornish Charters', in Gallagher, Roberts, and Tinti (eds.), *The Languages of Early Medieval Charters*, 342–77.

Ireland, Colin, 'Aldfrith of Northumbria and the Irish Genealogies', *Celtica* 22 (1991): 64–88.

Insley, Charles, 'Archives and Lay Documentary Practice in the Anglo-Saxon World', in W. C. Brown, M. Costambeys, M. Innes and A. J. Kosto (eds.), *Documentary Culture and the Laity in the Early Middle Ages* (Cambridge: Cambridge University Press, 2012), 336–62.

Ireland, Colin A., *The Gaelic Background of Old English Poetry before Bede* (Kalamazoo: Medieval Institute, 2022).

Jackson, Kenneth Hurlstone, *Language and History in Early Britain* (Edinburgh: Edinburgh University Press, 1953).

Jarman, Cat, *River Kings: A New History of the Vikings from Scandinavia to the Silk Roads* (London: William Collins, 2021).

Jefferson, Judith A. and Ad Putter (eds.) with Amanda Hopkins (asst.), *Multilingualism in Medieval Britain (c. 1066–1520): Sources and Analysis* (Turnhout: Brepols, 2013).

Jolly, Karen Louise, *Popular Religion in Late Saxon England: Elf Charms in Context* (Chapel Hill: University of North Carolina Press, 1996).

Jones, Nia Wyn [originally published as O. Wyn Jones], *Historical Writing in Medieval Wales* (Unpublished Ph.D. Thesis, Bangor University, 2013).

Jones, Nia Wyn [originally published as O. Wyn Jones], 'The Most Excellent Princes: Geoffrey of Monmouth and Medieval Welsh Historical Writing', in Joshua Byron Smith and Georgia Henley (eds.), *A Companion to Geoffrey of Monmouth* (Leiden: Brill, 2020), 257–90.

Joshel, Sandra R., *Slavery in the Roman World* (Cambridge: Cambridge University Press, 2010).

Jurasinski, Stefan, 'The *Rime of King William* and its Analogues', *Neophilologus* 88 (2004): 131–44.

Kapović, Mate (ed.), *The Indo-European Language*, 2nd ed. (Abingdon: Routledge, 2017).

Keefer, S. Larratt and D. R. Burrows, 'Hebrew and the *Hebraicum* in Late Anglo-Saxon England', *Anglo-Saxon England* 19 (1990): 67–80.

Kosto, Adam J., *Hostages in the Middle Ages* (Oxford: Oxford University Press, 2012).

Lancaster, Lorraine, 'Kinship in Anglo-Saxon Society', *British Journal of Sociology* 9 (1958): 230–49.

Lane, Alan and Mark Redknap, *Llangorse Crannog: The Excavation of an Early Medieval Royal Site in the Kingdom of Brycheiniog* (Oxford: Oxbow Books, 2019).

Lapidge, Michael, 'The School of Theodore and Hadrian', *Anglo-Saxon England* 15 (1986): 45–72.

Lapidge, Michael (ed.), *Interpreters of Early Medieval Britain* (Oxford: Oxford University Press for The British Academy, 2002).

Lapidge, Michael and David Dumville (eds.), *Gildas: New Approaches* (Woodbridge: The Boydell Press, 1984).

Lavelle, Ryan and Simon Roffey (eds.), *Danes in Wessex: The Scandinavian Impact on Southern England, c.800–c.1100* (Oxford: Oxbow, 2016).

Lendinara, Patrizia, 'The World of Anglo-Saxon Learning', in Malcolm Godden and Michael Lapidge (eds.), *The Cambridge Companion to Old English Literature* (Cambridge: Cambridge University Press, 1986), 264–81.

Lendinara, Patrizia, *Anglo-Saxon Glosses and Glossaries* (Aldershot: Ashgate, 1999).

Lindsay, W. M., *The Corpus, Épinal, Erfurt and Leyden Glossaries* (London: Oxford University Press, 1921).

Loyn, Henry, *The Vikings in Britain* (Oxford: Blackwell, 1994).

Major, Tristan, *Undoing Babel: The Tower of Babel in Anglo-Saxon Literature* (Toronto: University of Toronto Press, 2018).

McCann, Sarah, *Bede's 'Plures De Scottorum Regione': The Irish in the 'Historia Ecclesiastica Gentis Anglorum'* (Unpublished Ph.D. Thesis, National University of Ireland, Galway, 2013).

McKie, Michael, 'The Origins and Early Development of Rhyme in English Verse', *The Modern Language Review* 92 (1997): 817–31.

Meroney, Howard, 'Irish in the Old English Charms', *Speculum* 20 (1945): 172–82.

Merrills, A. H., *History and Geography in Late Antiquity* (Cambridge: Cambridge University Press, 2005).

Miller, D. Gary, *External Influences on English: From Its Beginnings to the Renaissance* (Oxford: Oxford University Press, 2012).

Molyneaux, George, '*The Ordinance Concerning the Dunsæte* and the Welsh Frontier in the Late Tenth and Eleventh Centuries', *Anglo-Saxon England* 40 (2012): 249–72.

Mostert, Marco, 'Linguistics of Contact in the Northern Seas', in Rolf Strootman, Floris van den Eijnde, and Roy van Wijk (eds.), *Empires of the Sea: Maritime Power Networks in World History* (Leiden: Brill, 2020), 179–93.

Mullen, Alex, *Southern Gaul and the Mediterranean: Multilingualism and Multiple Identities in the Iron Age and Roman Periods* (Cambridge: Cambridge University Press, 2019).

Naismith, Rory, *Early Medieval Britain c. 500–1000* (Cambridge: Cambridge University Press, 2021).

Naismith, Rory, 'Bige Habban: An Introduction to Money, Trade and Cross-Border Traffic', *Offa's Dyke Journal* 4 (2022): 16–35.

Naismith, Rory and David A. Woodman (eds.), *Writing, Kingship and Power in Anglo-Saxon England* (Cambridge: Cambridge University Press, 2018).

Ní Chatháin, Próinséas, 'Bede's Ecclesiastical History in Irish', *Peritia* 3 (1984): 115–30.

Olsen, K. E., A. Harbus, and T. Hofstra, *Germanic Texts and Latin Models: Medieval Reconstructions* (Leuven: Peeters, 2001).

Ní Mhaonaigh, Máire, 'Of Bede's "Five Languages and Four Nations": The Earliest Writing from Ireland, Scotland and Wales', in C. Lees (ed.), *The Cambridge History of Early Medieval English Literature* (Cambridge: Cambridge University Press, 2012), 99–119.

Owen-Crocker, Gale R., 'Brides, Donors, Traders: Imports into Anglo-Saxon England', in Angela Ling Huang and Carsten Jahnke (eds.), *Textiles and the Medieval Economy: Production, Trade and Consumption of Textiles, 8th–16th Centuries* (Oxford: Oxbow Books, 2015), 64–77.

Padel, O. J., *Cornish Place-Name Elements* (Nottingham: English Place-Name Society, 1985).

Padel, Oliver, *Slavery in Saxon Cornwall: The Bodmin Manumissions*, Kathleen Hughes Memorial Lectures 7 (Cambridge: Department of Anglo-Saxon, Norse and Celtic, 2009).

Parry-Williams, T. H., *The English Element in Welsh: A Study of English Loan-Words in Welsh* (London: Honourable Society of Cymmrodorion, 1923).

Parsons, David, 'Place-Names and Offa's Dyke: The Limits of Inference', *Offa's Dyke Journal* 4 (2022): 107–31.

Patterson, Nick, et al., 'Large-Scale Migration into Britain during the Middle to Late Bronze Age', *Nature* 601 (2021): 588–94.

Pelteret, David A. E., *Slavery in Early Mediaeval England: From the Reign of Alfred until the Twelfth Century* (Woodbridge: The Boydell Press, 1995).

Pettitt, Paul and Mark White, *The British Palaeolithic: Hominin Societies at the Edge of the Pleistocene World* (Abingdon: Routledge, 2012).

Pheifer, J. D., 'Early Anglo-Saxon Glossaries and the School of Canterbury', *Anglo-Saxon England* 16 (1987): 17–44.

Pons-Sanz, Sara M., *Norse-Derived Vocabulary in Late Old English Texts: Wulfstan's Works, a Case Study* (Amsterdam: University Press of Southern Denmark, 2007).

Price, Jonathan J., Margalit Finkelberg, and Yuval Shahar (eds.), *Rome: An Empire of Many Nations: New Perspectives on Ethnic Diversity and Cultural Identity* (Cambridge: Cambridge University Press, 2021).

Pryce, Huw, *Writing Welsh History from the Early Middle Ages to the Twenty-First Century* (Oxford: Oxford University Press, 2022).

Rio, Alice, *Slavery after Rome, 500–1100* (Oxford: Oxford University Press, 2017).

Robinson, Fred C., '"The Rewards of Piety": Two Old English Poems in Their Manuscript Context', in Patrick J. Gallacher and Helen Damico (eds.), *Hermeneutics and Medieval Culture* (Albany: State University of New York Press, 1989), 193–200.

Robinson, Orrin W., *Old English and Its Closest Relatives: A Survey of the Earliest Germanic Languages* (London: Routledge, 1992).

Rowley, Sharon M., *The Old English Version of Bede's Historia Ecclesiastica* (Cambridge: D. S. Brewer, 2011).

Russell, Paul, *Between Ogam and Runes: The So-Called 'Alphabet of Nemnivus'*, Lecture at University of Notre Dame, January 2016.

Russell, Paul, *Reading Ovid in Medieval Wales* (Columbus: The Ohio State University Press, 2017).

Russell, Paul, 'Two Notes on *Historia Brittonum*', *Cambrian Medieval Celtic Studies* 84 (2022): 41–9.

Salway, Peter, *A History of Roman Britain* (Oxford: Oxford University Press, 1993; repr. 2001).

Sawyer, P. H., *From Roman Britain to Norman England* (London: Methuen, 1978).

Scahill, John, 'Trilingualism in Early Middle English Miscellanies: Languages and Literature', *The Yearbook of English Studies* 33 (2003): 18–32.

Scheil, Andrew P., *The Footsteps of Israel: Understanding Jews in Anglo-Saxon England* (Ann Arbor: The University of Michigan Press, 2004).

Schrijver, Peter, 'What Britons Spoke around 400 AD', in Higham (ed.), *Britons in Anglo-Saxon England*, 165–71.

Schrijver, Peter, *Language Contact and the Origins of the Germanic Languages* (Abingdon: Routledge, 2014).

Seiler, Annina, 'Germanic Names, Vernacular Sounds, and Latin Spellings in Early Anglo-Saxon and Alemannic Charters', in Gallagher, Roberts, and Tinti (eds.), *The Languages of Early Medieval Charters*, 117–53.

Sims-Williams, Patrick, *The Celtic Inscriptions of Britain: Phonology and Chronology, c.400–1200* (Oxford: Blackwell, 2003).

Sims-Williams, Patrick, *Irish Influence on Medieval Welsh Literature* (Oxford: Oxford University Press, 2011).

Smith, D. K., *The Cartographic Imagination in Early Modern England: Rewriting the World in Marlowe, Spenser, Raleigh and Marvell* (Aldershot: Ashgate, 2008).

Stafford, Pauline, *After Alfred: Anglo-Saxon Chronicles & Chroniclers, 900–1150* (Oxford: Oxford University Press, 2020).

Stanton, Robert, *The Culture of Translation in Anglo-Saxon England* (Cambridge: D. S. Brewer, 2002).

Stephenson, Rebecca and Emily V. Thornbury (eds.), *Latinity and Identity in Anglo-Saxon Literature* (Toronto: University of Toronto Press, 2016).

Story, Joanna, 'Charlemagne and the Anglo-Saxons', in Joanna Story (ed.), *Charlemagne: Empire and Society* (Manchester: Manchester University Press, 2005), 195–210.

Suppe, Frederick C., 'Who Was Rhys Sais? Some Comments on Anglo-Welsh Relations before 1066', *Haskins Society Journal* 7 (1995): 63–73.

Suppe, Frederick C., 'Interpreter Families and Anglo-Welsh Relations in the Shropshire- Powys Marches in the Twelfth Century', *Anglo-Norman Studies: Proceedings of the Battle Conference* 30 (2007): 196–212.

Thomas, Hugh M., *The Norman Conquest: England after William the Conqueror* (Lanham: Rowman & Littlefield, 2008).

Thomas, Rebecca, 'Ysytr *anghyfiaith* mewn testunau Cymraeg Canol', *Studia Celtica* 55 (2021): 75–96.

Thomas, Rebecca, *History and Identity in Early Medieval Wales* (Woodbridge: D. S. Brewer, 2022).

Tinti, Francesca, *Europe and the Anglo-Saxons*, Cambridge Elements (Cambridge: Cambridge University Press, 2021).

Townend, Matthew, 'Cnut's Poets: An Old Norse Literary Community in Eleventh-Century England', in Tyler (ed.), *Conceptualizing Multilingualism in England*, 197–215.

Townend, Matthew, 'Contextualizing the *Knútsdrápur*: Skaldic Praise-Poetry at the Court of Cnut', *Anglo-Saxon England* 30 (2001): 145–79.

Townend, Matthew, *Language and History in Viking Age England: Linguistic Relations between Speakers of Old Norse and Old English* (Turnhout: Brepols, 2002).

Townend, Matthew (ed.), *Wulfstan, Archbishop of York: The Proceedings of the Second Alcuin Conference* (Turnhout: Brepols, 2004).

Treharne, Elaine, *Living through Conquest: The Politics of Early English, 1020 to 1220* (Oxford: Oxford University Press, 2012).

Trotter, D. A. (ed.), *Multilingualism in Later Medieval Britain* (Cambridge: D. S. Brewer, 2000).

Tyler, Elizabeth M. (ed.), *Conceptualizing Multilingualism in England, c.800–c.1250* (Turnhout: Brepols, 2011).

Valtonen, Irmeli, *The North in the Old English Orosius: A Geographical Narrative in Context* (Helsinki: Société Néophilologique, 2008).

Versloot, Arjen P., 'Traces of a North Sea Germanic Idiom in the Fifth-Seventh Centuries AD', in Hines and IJssennagger-van der Pluijm, *Frisians of the Early Middle Ages*, 339–73.

Ward-Perkins, Bryan, 'Why Did the Anglo-Saxons Not Become More British?', *The English Historical Review* 115 (2000): 513–33.

Williams, Ann, *The English and the Norman Conquest* (Woodbridge: The Boydell Press, 1995).

Williams, Gareth, 'Kingship, Christianity, and Coinage: Monetary and Political Perspectives on Silver Economy in the Viking Age', in James Graham-Campbell and Gareth Williams (eds.), *Silver Economy in the Viking Age* (Walnut Creek: Left Coast Press, 2007), 177–214.

Wilson, Andrew and Alan Bowman (eds.), *Trade, Commerce, and the State in the Roman World* (Oxford: Oxford University Press, 2018).

Wilson, Stephen, *The Means of Naming: A Social and Cultural History of Personal Naming in Western Europe* (London: UCL Press, 1998).

Wogan-Browne, Jocelyn, 'General Introduction: What's in a Name: The "French" of "England"', in Wogan-Browne, et al. (eds.), *The French of England*, 1–13.

Wogan-Browne, Jocelyn, et al. (eds.), *Language and Culture in Medieval Britain: The French of England, c.1100–c.1500* (New York: York Medieval Press, 2009).

Woolf, Alex, 'Apartheid Economics in Anglo-Saxon England', in Higham (ed.), *Britons in Anglo-Saxon England*, 115–29.

Woolf, Alex, *From Pictland to Alba, 789–1070* (Edinburgh: Edinburgh University Press, 2007).

Wormald, Patrick, *The Making of English Law: King Alfred to the Twelfth Century* (Oxford: Blackwell, 1999).

Wyatt, David, *Slaves and Warriors in Medieval Britain and Ireland, 800–1200* (Leiden: Brill, 2009).

Yorke, Barbara, *Kings and Kingdoms of Early Anglo-Saxon England* (London: Routledge, 1990).

Zweck, Jordan, *Epistolary Acts: Anglo-Saxon Letters and Early English Media* (Toronto: University of Toronto Press, 2018).

Acknowledgements

I am grateful to Megan Cavell, Marios Costambeys, and the two anonymous readers of this manuscript for thoughtful suggestions that have improved this volume.

Cambridge Elements ☰

England in the Early Medieval World

Megan Cavell
University of Birmingham

Megan Cavell is Associate Professor in medieval English literature at the University of Birmingham. She works on a wide range of topics in medieval literary studies, from Old and early Middle English and Latin languages and literature to riddling, gender and animal studies. Her previous publications include *Weaving Words and Binding Bodies: The Poetics of Human Experience in Old English Literature* (2016), *Riddles at Work in the Early Medieval Tradition: Words, Ideas, Interactions* (co-edited with Jennifer Neville, 2020), and *The Medieval Bestiary in England: Texts and Translations of the Old and Middle English Physiologus* (2022)

Rory Naismith
University of Cambridge

Rory Naismith is Professor of Early Medieval English History in the Department of Anglo-Saxon, Norse and Celtic at the University of Cambridge, and a Fellow of Corpus Christi College, Cambridge. Also a Fellow of the Royal Historical Society, he is the author of *Early Medieval Britain 500–1000* (Cambridge University Press, 2021), *Citadel of the Saxons: The Rise of Early London* (2018), *Medieval European Coinage, with a Catalogue of the Coins in the Fitzwilliam Museum, Cambridge, 8: Britain and Ireland c. 400–1066* (Cambridge University Press, 2017) and *Money and Power in Anglo-Saxon England: The Southern English Kingdoms 757–865* (Cambridge University Press, 2012, which won the 2013 International Society of Anglo-Saxonists First Book Prize).

Winfried Rudolf
University of Göttingen

Winfried Rudolf is Chair of Medieval English Language and Literature in the University of Göttingen (Germany). Recent publications include *Childhood and Adolescence in Anglo-Saxon Literary Culture* (with Susan E. Irvine, 2018). He has published widely on homiletic literature in early England and is currently principal investigator of the ERC-Project ECHOE–Electronic Corpus of Anonymous Homilies in Old English.

Emily V. Thornbury
Yale University

Emily V. Thornbury is Associate Professor of English at Yale University. She studies the literature and art of early England, with a particular emphasis on English and Latin poetry. Her publications include *Becoming a Poet in Anglo-Saxon England* (Cambridge, 2014), and, co-edited with Rebecca Stephenson, *Latinity and Identity in Anglo-Saxon Literature* (2016). She is currently working on a monograph called *The Virtue of Ornament*, about pre-Conquest theories of aesthetic value.

About the Series

Elements in England in the Early Medieval World takes an innovative, interdisciplinary view of the culture, history, literature, archaeology, and legacy of England between the fifth and eleventh centuries. Individual contributions question and situate key themes, and thereby bring new perspectives to the heritage of early medieval England.
They draw on texts in Latin and Old English as well as material culture to paint a vivid picture of the period. Relevant not only to students and scholars working in medieval studies, these volumes explore the rich intellectual, methodological, and comparative value that the dynamic researchers interested in England between the fifth and eleventh centuries have to offer in a modern, global context. The series is driven by a commitment to inclusive and critical scholarship, and to the view that early medieval studies have a part to play in many fields of academic research, as well as constituting a vibrant and self-contained area of research in its own right.

Cambridge Elements ≡

England in the Early Medieval World

Printed in the United States
by Baker & Taylor Publisher Services